What people are saying about

Jumping Sharks and Dropping Mics

An absolute delight: I wish I'd written it myself! The range of applications in new contexts is second to none. It blends etymology, social history and current usage, bringing together a wealth of British and American examples

David Crystal, author of *The Stories* *t's Talk, How Language Works*, and many m

Who knew there were ~~areth Carrol has brought the idiom~~ ~~ate and assembled a light-hearted and info~~ ~~sure trove of expressions that we may well know, ~~ ~~nose origin we might not have thought about. I've learnt so much from this book, which is sure to extend any reader's knowledge of the English language.

Alison Wray, Professor of Language and Communication, Cardiff University, UK

Smart, funny and crammed full of fascinating facts. The perfect book for word nerds everywhere.

Gavin Extence, author of *The Universe Versus Alex Woods*

Confronting what we take for granted in what we read, hear, write and say is not an easy job, but this book does it with precision. The devil, as they say, is in the detail, and the inherent charm of the English language's near-countless set pieces is forensically – but affectionately – laid bare. The highlights are the quirks of the sporting lexicon – from hairdryers to squeaky bum time – the examinations of which will make more than a few football writers question the world they live in.

Adam Hurrey, author of *Football Clichés*

Gareth Carrol gives us an expert's tour of the hotspots where popular culture meets etymology. A rich dive into the wheres, whys, and hows of linguistic memes.

Lynne Murphy, author of *The Prodigal Tongue* and Professor of Linguistics, University of Sussex, UK

Jumping Sharks and Dropping Mics

Modern idioms and where they come from

Jumping Sharks and Dropping Mics

Modern idioms and where they come from

Gareth Carrol

IFF
BOOKS

Winchester, UK
Washington, USA

JOHN HUNT PUBLISHING

First published by iff Books, 2021
iff Books is an imprint of John Hunt Publishing Ltd., No. 3 East Street, Alresford,
Hampshire SO24 9EE, UK
office@jhpbooks.com
www.johnhuntpublishing.com
www.iff-books.com

For distributor details and how to order please visit the 'Ordering' section on our website.

ISBN: 978 1 78904 856 8
978 1 78904 857 5 (ebook)
Library of Congress Control Number: 2021930345

A CIP catalogue record for this book is available from the British Library.

Design: Stuart Davies

UK: Printed and bound by CPI Group (UK) Ltd, Croydon, CR0 4YY
Printed in North America by CPI GPS partners

We operate a distinctive and ethical publishing philosophy in
all areas of our business, from our global network of authors to
production and worldwide distribution.

Contents

For Abi, for everything.

Preface

The idea for this book first sprang into life not long after I started working at the University of Birmingham in 2016. As part of a class on "Ordinary Creativity", I included an activity asking students to think of examples of phrases they used in their everyday lives that had emerged from popular culture. The session was immensely enjoyable, and also introduced me to several idioms that have ended up in this book that I had never heard before. It also served to prove what I already suspected: that there are plenty of examples of idioms that we can trace directly to TV shows, movies and other "modern" sources that are now firmly embedded in the language, regardless of whether people realise where they come from.

Over the next few years I gathered examples that I felt fitted the idiomatic bill, and an article written for the language magazine *Babel* in 2019 acted as a precursor to this book. I settled on the format – entries of around 500 words – on the grounds that this allows me to both tell the story of an idiom and pick out illustrative examples of how it has come to be used. The end result is, I hope, an interesting tour through some of the phrases that are now very much a part of modern English. Readers may not be familiar with all of the entries, but I hope that everyone picking this up will learn at least one new phrase by the end of it, and will certainly learn a bit more about the (sometimes surprising) origins of phrases they already know and use.

I am grateful to several people for their help with this project. Firstly, thanks to my wife, Abi Rhodes, and my friend and colleague, Jeannette Littlemore, who both read through full drafts and offered encouraging feedback throughout. Thanks also to (in no particular order): Janine Forster, Richard Dawson, Charlotte Ball, Sadie Scott, Tom Hemingway, Jen Hill, Dan Malt, Thurstan Russell, Bodo Winter and Adam Schembri, all of whom offered feedback on particular sections of the book, suggested candidates for inclusion, or generally helped out with enjoyable and incredibly useful conversations about the idea.

Gareth Carrol, November 2020

1

Introduction: Why Can't People Just Say What They Mean?

I know all those words, but that sentence makes no sense to me.
Matt Groening

Idioms form an important part of our everyday vocabulary, even if we don't realise it. On a regular basis we might *spill the beans* or *drop the ball*, causing someone to *hit the roof* and there may be *Hell to pay* as a result. Hopefully, sooner or later they may have a *change of heart*, we *bury the hatchet* and *wipe the slate clean*, and no one is the *worse for wear*. The origins of these, and many more, everyday phrases are unknown to most, but it doesn't stop us using them freely and frequently as a way of spicing up our interactions. In many cases, especially in context, the meaning is more or less self-explanatory. For example, a phrase like *drop the ball* largely speaks for itself, since dropping something is rarely good, especially in sporting terms. In plenty of other cases, though, phrases that we may use and understand without a second thought may seem much less obvious when (and if!) we stop to think about why they mean what they do. For instance, why do people who steel themselves to do something *bite the bullet*? Why do we *pull someone's leg* if we want to tease them? And what on earth does *kicking the bucket* have to do with dying?

This last example is the one most commonly used to demonstrate the curious nature of idioms. A large part of the problem here is that we can't work out the meaning of many such phrases simply by trying to break them down into their component words (what linguists would call the "non-decomposable" nature of idioms). Alongside *kick the bucket*, other prime examples in English include *cut the mustard* (to do something very well or meet expectations), *shoot the breeze* (to chat casually with someone), and several more referring to death or dying such as *pop your clogs*, *buy the farm* and *bite the dust*, to name just a few that, on the face of it, make very little sense at all. When such phrases are already known to us they present few problems (most people simply know that *kick the bucket* means "die"), but for others, the sentiment expressed by creator of *The Simpsons*, Matt Groening, at the start of this chapter will be all too familiar. For idioms we have never heard before, it may be that we recognise all of the words being used but have no idea what they mean when they are combined in certain ways.

Idioms are not all the same, however, and at least some seem fairly easy to work out once it is recognised that the meaning is not literal. Whilst a phrase like *kick the bucket* may seem relatively impenetrable, an example like *at the end of the day* may be much easier to interpret. Here *day* refers metaphorically to any situation or discussion at hand, hence the leap of understanding required is relatively small. Other examples fall somewhere in the middle: a phrase like *spill the beans* is straightforward because we can easily interpret *spill* to mean "reveal" even if we don't automatically assume that *beans* should mean "secret". Often there may be clues like this that we can draw on to help us infer a meaning, and metaphor is an important aspect of how we interpret many idioms. When linguists talk about metaphors they simply mean "describing one thing in terms of another", so saying something like *my boss is a monster* would be just as much a metaphor as something more literary like *Juliet is the Sun*. Some linguists talk about universal ideas or "conceptual metaphors" that seem to shape the way we talk and think, even if we don't realise it. A common example might be the idea that LIFE IS A JOURNEY (conceptual metaphors are, by convention, written in capital letters), which in turn gives us phrases like *reaching a crossroads* in our lives, *moving on* after an unpleasant experience, or *crossing that bridge when we come to it*. For some idioms, we might therefore be able to identify conceptual metaphors that help us to work out the meaning, such as examples like *hit the roof*, *blow your top* or *let off steam*, all of which seem to reflect the idea that ANGER IS PRESSURE. Similarly, phrases like *over the moon, on top of the world* or *walking on air* all seem to reflect a metaphor like HAPPY IS UP, and, conversely, SAD IS DOWN gives us phrases like *down in the dumps*, have a *sinking feeling* or simply *feeling low*.

Other types of idiom only make sense if we have the required background knowledge, since they point to specific areas or domains of experience and may therefore be difficult to understand if you don't see the reference. Examples in English include phrases such as *throw in the towel* or *on the ropes*, which most people will recognise as meaning, respectively, "give up" and "be in a disadvantageous position". People may or may not know that these come from the world of boxing, but not having this information doesn't stop anyone from using or understanding these phrases. Boxing, like many other sports, contributes a number of such idioms to English (see Chapter 5), as do domains in English such as seafaring (*all hands on deck, batten down the hatches, a loose cannon, know/learn the ropes* and *by and large*), reflecting its historical and cultural importance in the English speaking world. In the same way, idioms in other languages can give us important insights into the culture and history of the people who use them: German, for instance, has several idioms involving pigs, reflecting the importance of this particular animal to the German people.[1]

All of these examples help us to see why some idioms may be much less obvious than others. When an original cultural reference is not known or recognised, the phrase may seem very unclear compared to more transparent phrases such as those underpinned by more general metaphors. *Throw in the towel* is a good example, since the phrase has come to mean "give up" generally, and not simply in the context of boxing, where the action of throwing a towel into the ring is taken as a signal that a fighter's support team wants to concede on her or his behalf. Such "iconic" phrases – where a symbolic action is extended and applied more generally than its original use – are common, and these may be the idioms that seem the most nonsensical when we stop to think about them. Another good example is the phrase *bury the hatchet*, which originally referenced a symbolic act of peace amongst Native Americans whereby warring tribes would sometimes bury their weapons as a way of marking the end of a period of hostility. As with so many other examples, knowing or not knowing this doesn't affect our ability to use the idiom, and in some cases (as demonstrated by more than one student in the past), people may be familiar with the phrase without having any clue what a hatchet even is!

Often, these are also the phrases most prone to the process of "folk etymology", where language users may come up with incredibly creative, very sensible, but fundamentally wrong explanations for where the meaning actually comes from. *Kick the bucket* is again a prime example, and many people (linguists included) wrongly assume that the bucket in question probably refers to an upturned bucket on which a to-be-hanged person might stand, hence kicking this away would lead to a short, sharp drop to her or his death. Several problems exist with this, however (why would anyone be standing on a bucket, of all things?), not least the fact that there is no historical evidence to suggest that it is the case. More convincing (although still open to debate) is the idea that the phrase dates back to the 16th century, when bucket had the additional dialect meaning of "wooden beam" or "yoke".[2] When animals were slaughtered, common practice would be to tie them up by their feet, then in their death throes they would spasm and kick against the "bucket" they were tied to. If this explanation is true, we have another example of a specific action becoming more generally applied over time (just like *throw in the towel*), with the additional complication that in this case, the dialect meaning of bucket has all but disappeared from English, making the link between the phrase and a modern reading of the words unclear. Extreme cases of this can even result in people coming up with logical explanations for phrases that are actually misheard in the first place. In British English a common example of this is the often misused *damp squid*, meaning something that is disappointing and underwhelming. The phrase is actually *damp squib*, and once we know that a squib is an old-fashioned type of firework, we can understand why a damp one might not perform as well as we might hope. A *damp squid*, on the other hand, if we stop to think about it, should be nothing unusual at all, given that most squids spend most of their lives in water. Such examples – sometimes called "eggcorns" – demonstrate our tendency to learn and use words and phrases throughout our lives without really giving much thought to why they might mean what they do.

Just like individual words, idioms emerge and die out in language. Some idioms seem very old-fashioned and may only be understood by speakers of a certain vintage, such as the English euphemism for going to the toilet, *spend a penny*. In the UK public toilets, historically, had coin-operated locks that cost a penny to get in, so the link would have seemed obvious at the time, but since the practice is no longer common the reference is unlikely to resonate with most, and the idiom seems to be on its way out for this reason. Hundreds if not thousands of phrases have probably disappeared from the language in the same way, and many may survive only in historical fiction or works attempting to recreate the language of days gone by. In particular, British author Georgette Heyer was adept at including many authentic (but now largely obsolete) examples of English slang from the Regency period in her historical fiction, such as the archaic examples *draw someone's cork* (to punch someone in the nose) and *properly shot in the neck* (to be drunk).[3]

The focus of this book is not those idioms that have dropped out of usage, but the exact opposite: those that have entered our language in recent decades from a variety of "modern" avenues. One big advantage here is that in the digital information age, detailed records mean that in many cases we can track new coinages very closely, and thereby identify the origin of many new idioms in a way that simply isn't possible for older, more established phrases. In this way, we can chart the emergence of phrases from a range of sources, identifying (in many cases) a fairly clear origin for some of the idioms that have come into the language only relatively recently. "Modern" here is a fairly flexible term, and the phrases considered mostly date from the second half of the 20th century onward, with a handful creeping just a little further back in time. Some may have an earlier first usage, but only show signs of starting to spread and become more popular later on. Entries are organised thematically, covering TV, movies, the Internet, sports, literature, and a miscellaneous set of general phrases, but all are relative newcomers to the English language.

Similarly, the exact description of what constitutes an idiom is relatively broad. In linguistic terms, an idiom is a phrase whose meaning is not derived simply from the meanings of the individual words. However, this may be true of many types of phrase (metaphors, for example), and some degree of fixedness and familiarity amongst users of the language is also characteristic of most idioms (in other words, an idiom is a set phrase, and likely to be recognised by most speakers within any given speech community). In this collection, three primary characteristics are considered to constitute idiom-hood. The first is, by necessity, that all entries must consist of more than one individual word. In one or two examples even this designation becomes a little loose, but the use of hyphens and a bit of artistic licence means that at worst, they are borderline cases rather than out-and-out exceptions to the rule. For linguists, the definition of a "word" is a tricky one at the best of times, and some of the entries may even appear in dictionaries or other collections of newly coined "words", but such a quibble should not detract too much from the examples outlined here.

The second characteristic is that, like the vast majority of idioms, all of the phrases here have two potential meanings: an entirely literal reading, and a figurative meaning that is not immediately obvious from the phrase itself. Whilst some idioms require a bit of creative manipulation to think of a suitable literal interpretation (can you literally be *over the moon*?), the point remains that the figurative meanings of all of the entries here are, generally speaking, not predictable without some additional knowledge or background information.

The third aspect of vital importance is that all of these modern idioms have (to a greater or lesser degree) gone beyond their original contexts of use and entered into wider circulation. In some cases this might be a relatively small leap (see Chapter 5, for examples of idioms that have crossed from one sport to another), but others demonstrate more expansive journeys into the vocabulary at large, as with examples throughout the collection. The relative familiarity of all of these idioms is confirmed by uses of their figurative sense in newspaper articles, online forums or other platforms, even if they may not yet be as widespread and well-known as some of the more "classic" idioms discussed earlier in this chapter.

Idioms are worth studying for many reasons, not least because of the cultural trends they often reflect, and one of the joys of researching in this particular area is the fun that can be had in learning about odd-sounding phrases and where they come from. The aim of this book is primarily to introduce a set of phrases that readers will (hopefully) find interesting and entertaining, and although readers may disagree with some of the entries – in terms of their importance, their origin, or even their status as idioms – at the very least, there should be something in here for everyone.

A word on sources

Throughout this book, references to a number of online sources are made, to help support the explanations and origins being proposed, and to demonstrate the ways in which different phrases have come to be used in the wider world. Where possible, links to all sources are provided and the majority were, at the time of writing, free to access, should any reader want to follow these up and learn more. (For anything behind a paywall, publication details are provided.) Of particular use are The Phrase Finder, for information on many English idioms; language blogs such as Word Histories, Word Origins, Grammarphobia and Grammarist; websites TV Tropes and Know Your Meme; and, as they relate to slang, The Big Apple and the ever-useful Urban Dictionary. More established dictionary authorities referred to include Oxford Dictionaries, Macmillan, Merriam-Webster, Dictionary.com and The Free Dictionary.

One final source that helps us to investigate the development of words and phrases is the Google Books Ngrams Viewer (an "Ngram" is a sequence of words, when "n" tells us the number of words). This tool allows us to track the usage of a word or phrase in printed literature during the past 500 years or so, giving us a useful indication of when a phrase might begin to show an upsurge in popularity. Whilst there are limits to what this can tell us (for one, appearance in print is likely to come only once a phrase is already well on its way to being recognised more widely), it at least lends weight to judgments about when and where a particular modern idiom may have started to spread its wings. Throughout this book, when an entry talks of an increase in usage, this is the kind of data that such a judgment is based on.

Taken together, the information that can be readily found online can be used to piece together a reliable account of when, how and in some cases even why a phrase entered the wider language. The other sources that are referenced – newspaper and magazine articles, blog posts and excerpts from recorded interviews – give us all the evidence we need of just how widespread some of these phrases have become.

2

Don't Touch that Dial: Idioms from the World of TV

Of all the great inventions of the 20th century, few things can claim to have had the cultural impact of television. Early experiments in broadcasting began during the 1930s, but the first regular TV shows did not appear until the late 1940s, sparking what came to be called the "Golden Age of Television" in the USA. Notable early examples include the anthology drama series *Kraft Television Theatre* (premiered 7th May 1947), which presented viewers with live television plays on a weekly basis for over ten years, and the first televised variety show, *Texaco Star Theater* (premiered 8th June 1948), hosted by Milton "Mr Television" Berle. Generally regarded as an era of high-brow broadcasting, the "Golden Age" lasted until the late 1950s, by which time both technology and viewing habits were changing rapidly. Early sitcoms (often developed from existing radio programmes) emerged as early as 1946: UK show *Pinwright's Progress* is regarded as the first ever TV sitcom, with *Mary Kay and Johnny* following in the USA in 1947. By the 1950s the genre really took off, with iconic shows such as *I Love Lucy* (which began airing in 1951), *The Honeymooners* (1955) and, in the UK, *Hancock's Half Hour* (1956) paving the way for what was to follow.

Fast forward 70 years or so and the scale and scope of modern broadcasts would make the medium unrecognisable to those early pioneers who were restricted to single cameras and live, warts and all broadcasts. TV occupied a central place in homes during the latter half of the 20th century, and although viewing habits are now quite different through on-demand and streaming services, the serial nature of so many of our favourite shows means that their place in the culture (and language) is assured. As a result, TV catchphrases are as much a part of our vocabulary as anything else. Some well-known examples from UK TV might include *I have a cunning plan* (Blackadder), *Am I bovvered?* (The Catherine Tate Show), *You stupid boy* or *don't panic!* (Dad's Army), *Don't mention the war!* (Fawlty Towers), *I'll get my coat* and *Does my bum look big in this?* (The Fast Show), and any number of other gems that have gained cult status amongst comedy fans everywhere. From US TV, catchphrases like *I love it when a plan comes together* (The A-Team), *What you talkin' 'bout, Willis?* (Diff'rent Strokes), *Danger, Will Robinson* (Lost in Space), *Just one more thing...* (Columbo) and countless others will be familiar to TV viewers of all ages, often delivered in the telltale style of the original line.

One show in particular that might lay claim to having had as much cultural legacy as any, at least in the last 25 years, is *Friends*, which ran for 236 episodes from 1994 to 2004 (and has been repeated almost non-stop since). Few shows have had the same level of enduring appeal as this sitcom following the lives and loves of six young New Yorkers, and the contribution to the language has been well documented.[1] As well as introducing one of TVs most memorable chat-up lines – Joey Tribbiani's *How you doin'?* – *Friends* is credited with popularising the concept of *the friend zone*, to describe a situation where one would-be romantic partner is seen by the other as simply a good friend rather than anything more amorous, *going commando* (not wearing underwear), and the idea of *being on a break* in a relationship. It also introduced a personal favourite: *a moo point* (a mis-hearing of "moot point"), explained as something that doesn't matter or, in other words, "a cow's opinion".

These examples (and many, many more) demonstrate the pervasive power of the TV catchphrase to enter the language we all use. The idioms considered in this chapter represent not just soundbites that are repeated for the joy of it, but ideas that have made the leap from the small screen into the wider world in a more expansive way.

Can I phone a friend?

An indication that someone requires help or advice addressing the issue in question.

Quiz show *Who Wants to Be a Millionaire?* (UK, 1998-2014; 2018-present; often shortened to *WWTBAM* or just *Millionaire*) first debuted in 1998 and became an instant classic, gracing UK TV screens for the next 15 years and leading to more than 100 franchised versions in countries around the world. The original format saw contestants tasked with answering 15 multiple choice questions of increasing difficulty, with correspondingly large cash prizes for each question successfully answered. To help them along the way, three lifelines were provided: ask the studio audience, who voted on the answer they thought was correct; 50:50, where two of the four possible answers were removed; and *phone a friend*, where the contestant could call a friend and ask for her or his help in selecting the correct answer. Despite multiple changes to the format, including a range of different lifelines employed in international versions of the show, *Can I phone a friend?* became one of the most iconic and well-known lines associated with *Who Wants to Be a Millionaire?* Whilst other catchphrases from quiz shows are also part of the broader language (*Is that your final answer?* also from *Millionaire* and *You are the Weakest Link* from the show of the same name representing two modern examples), the concept of *phoning a friend* when in need of help shows an upsurge in usage starting in the late 1990s, suggesting that the phrase did enter the wider consciousness in a fairly significant way.

As time went on some versions of the show attempted to counteract the unfair advantage of having a friend connected to the Internet by either retiring *phone a friend* completely and replacing it with a different lifeline (as in the US version), or ensuring that potential friends were monitored by members of production staff who physically sat with them to ensure that no additional help could be obtained by simply searching for answers online (as in the UK version). Before these, however, *phone a friend* provided several of the show's most talked about moments. One of the more famous examples, at least in the US version of the show, was John Carpenter, who in 1999 became the first winner of the top prize in any version of *Millionaire*. Carpenter cruised through the first 14 questions with minimal difficulty and didn't use any of his lifelines until the final question, when he chose to *phone a friend* and call his father, not to ask for help, but to inform him that he was about to win one million dollars. (He duly gave the correct answer and scooped the top prize, proving that his confidence was not at all misplaced.) A less successful story followed in 2000, again on US *Millionaire,* when an overconfident *phone a friend* cost contestant Rudy Reber a cool $228,000 by giving him an incorrect answer to the half-million question. Rather than walk away with $250,000, Reber trusted his friend (he later said, only because of how sure he sounded when answering) and, in a moment that must haunt both men, dropped back down to the $32,000 mark when his final answer was revealed to be wrong. Happily, there were no hard feelings, and Reber was incredibly gracious about his friend's mistake, saying simply, "He didn't do it maliciously."

As a broader idiom, *phone a friend* has become a way to indicate that a person requires assistance of some kind, often in response to a tricky question or particular problem. To cite just one example, when diplomat Kelly Craft was nominated to be the new US ambassador to the UN in 2019, one journalist suggested that "Craft won't be able to *phone a friend* during the greatest test of her career", referring to her upcoming Senate confirmation hearing to confirm her appointment.[2] The writer felt no need to mention *Millionaire*, suggesting that the phrase is firmly embedded in modern usage (and relatively transparent, to boot, even if people don't necessarily get the reference).

Computer says no

A situation where decisions are made based on computer-stored information rather than common sense, or where inflexibility prevents a seemingly straightforward resolution.

Computer says no started life as the punchline to a recurring sketch on *Little Britain* (UK, radio 2000-2002 and TV 2003-2007). This comedy sketch show, created by David Walliams and Matt Lucas, presented a spoof guide to British life through parodies of quintessentially British characters in a range of absurd situations. One example was the thoroughly bored and unhelpful customer service representative Carol Beer (played by Walliams), who plied her trade in various industries (in her first appearances she worked in a bank, then later as a travel agent and finally on a hospital reception). Her default response to any request – regardless of how straightforward or reasonable – was to type something into her computer and respond with *"computer says no"*, to signify that the request could not be granted and that her hands were tied. The phrase quickly made it into wider usage, aptly describing a range of situations where it feels as if unnecessary bureaucracy and red tape may be getting in the way of a common-sense solution, or at least preventing the possibility of discussing one with an actual human being.

For a time during the early 2000s, this particular attitude was felt to have become commonplace in the world of personal financial applications, where rather than a person sitting down and assessing the suitability of an applicant for a mortgage or loan as in the good old days of personal bank managers, a centralised credit score would be used, with little if any flexibility. One article from 2013 suggested that as well as devolving responsibility to faceless credit scoring agencies, with no right of reply in the event of an unsuccessful application, such a system also allows for the possibility that people with otherwise very good credit records may be rejected because of errors in their stored information, leading to examples where the *computer says no* in a situation when a simple conversation with a human being may quickly clear up a mistake or misunderstanding.[3] Alternative uses of *computer says no* might relate to over-officious filters or algorithms that automatically remove "offensive" content, regardless of the context. One prime example of this came from an incident reported in 2007, when the council planning department for the UK town of Rochdale failed to receive important emails from a resident objecting to his neighbour's planned extension.[4] The culprit was a computer filter that deemed the word "erection" to be obscene, meaning that the emails never made it in time for the protestations to be heard.

The *computer says no* attitude is now commonly understood to describe any situation where there is a perceived lack of flexibility or humanity to decisions that are being made. The potential problem of this was highlighted in *New Scientist* in 2015, in an article discussing the increasing automation of a range of roles, including ones that specialise in inherently grey areas such as dispute resolution or moral judgments.[5] The article does point to the rise in online resolution centres – such as eBay's in-house platform or the Swedish company Swiftcourt – as a way of settling disputes relating to online transactions as proof that such an approach can be hugely successful without ever having to involve costly human lawyers. Despite such advances, the demise of the outsourced call centre and the resurgence in "local banking" suggest that *computer says no* remains a widespread concern, at least in the hearts and minds of frustrated consumers everywhere.

Does what it says on the tin

Something that performs in precisely the way that it claims to.

A notable example as it comes not from a TV show but

from an advertisement, *does (exactly) what it says on the tin* first emerged as a slogan for Ronseal (a UK-based manufacturer of wood dyes and stains, paints and preservatives) in a TV advert in 1994. Ronseal's aim was to emphasise the simplicity and up-frontness of the products, and the original advert featured a man telling the audience everything it needed to know about "Ronseal Quick Drying Woodstain", concluding with the lines, "So if you've got wood to stain and you want it to dry quickly, use Ronseal Quick Drying Woodstain. *It does exactly what it says on the tin*." The adverts became a staple of UK commercial breaks during the late-1990s and into the 21st century, and the phrase is now more widely used to denote something that does precisely the job it claims to do (no more, no less).

Examples of the phrase in more general usage are common, including two from UK politician, and later Prime Minister, David Cameron. In 2004, before he became leader of the Conservative Party, Cameron declared that, "People are crying out for a kind of Ronseal politics – they want it to *do what it says on the tin*." Clearly just as much a fan of the idea once he was in office, he returned to the phrase to describe his coalition government with the Liberal Democrats when in 2013 he explained, "It is a Ronseal deal – *it does what it says on the tin*." One columnist pointed out that since this announcement came on the back of a series of increasingly muddled and contradictory policy decisions, it wasn't entirely clear what this was supposed to mean, asking Cameron to "clear up one small mystery: What does it *say on the tin*?"[6] Deputy Prime Minister Nick Clegg took the opportunity to join in when he quipped, "Ronseal deal? You could call it the unvarnished truth."

Does what it says on the tin is now listed in multiple dictionaries (including *the Oxford Dictionary of English Idioms*) as a common expression, and was immortalised in the title of a song by British pop singer Katie Melua in 2007. Some sources even use the adjective "Ronseal-esque", suggesting that the phrase is so well known that it can even be bypassed altogether. The Ronseal website addresses the origins of its strapline, suggesting that it is the third best known slogan of all time (according to research undertaken by the *Creative Review* in 2012). A similar poll from 2008 also placed *does what it says on the tin* as the third most commonly used slogan in everyday life by Britons, beaten only by "Good things come to those who wait" (Guinness) and "Every little helps" (Tesco).[7]

In 2015, Ronseal capitalised on the success of its famous slogan by issuing a faux-apology for the fact that it was now inaccurate, on the grounds that many of Ronseal's products no longer come in tins (as pointed out by an array of "eagle-eyed Tweeters"). On 17th April of that year, a full page advert appeared in British newspapers entitled "An apology", followed by "Ronseal: does exactly what it says on the rotund 203.48mm by 189.12mm vacuum-moulded white polypropylene copolymer 5 litre labelled bucket." The ad was supported by a video released online at the same time, showing Ronseal's efforts to accommodate the change to a more accurate slogan, such as two workers attempting to fit the now awkwardly long strapline on to the existing products. (Cue reference to another modern idiom, when one of the workers quips, "We're gonna need a bigger tin" – see *You're gonna need a bigger boat*, Chapter 3.) A week later Ronseal followed up their tongue-in-cheek offering with a second video – "An Apology for our Apology" – announcing a return to the original slogan, amended with an asterisk to clarify, "even if not every product is technically in a tin".

Gardening leave

A period where a person is suspended from a job; alternatively, a period of leave prior to starting a new job during which no employment is allowed.

To be on *gardening leave* is, euphemistically, to be suspended from your current job, hence to have little else to do with your time but to stay at home and tend the garden. The term originated in the UK civil service, where "special leave" could be granted for exceptional purposes. It has also been widely applied in sectors such as banking, where *gardening leave* refers to a situation where an employee is required to serve out a period of notice prior to starting a new job, but required to stay away from the workplace during such a period. Originally this may have been to ensure that employees leaving to take up a role at a competing business would not be taking up-to-date sensitive information with them, or to avoid any acts of sabotage (deliberate, or as a result of a half-hearted approach to a job that was soon to be ending).

In keeping with its civil service roots, TV comedy *Yes, Prime Minister* (UK, 1986-1988), which revolves around the machinations of the UK government, is generally credited with having introduced the term to a wider audience in a 1986 episode entitled "One of Us". In response to the revelation that a former government senior official was a Russian spy, and that current Cabinet Secretary, Humphrey Appleby, was part of the team responsible for investigating (and clearing) the man in question during a previous investigation, Prime Minister Jim Hacker threatens to send Appleby on *gardening leave* while a new investigation is carried out. In keeping with this, the term is now more commonly used as a euphemism for "suspended", either temporarily pending an investigation or prior to an employee being terminated altogether.

Outside of politics and business, *gardening leave* has been employed in the world of football, describing a situation when a manager is removed from a position despite still having time to run on a contract. Ally McCoist, then manager of Scottish club Rangers, was described as such when he was relieved of his duties in late 2014, as was Southend manager Phil Brown in 2018. An article on law in sport from 2014 explicitly highlights the right of clubs to place managers on *garden leave* rather than allow them to simply terminate a contract when a rival comes in with a more attractive offer.[8] The phrase is even used on the UK government website as part of its advice on employment rights, confirming that an employer may require an employee to stay away during a period of notice but that full pay and contractual benefits would still apply. *Gardening leave* also appears on multiple employment websites, highlighting both sides of the argument: that while it is a legitimate way to prevent workers running off to rivals with lucrative information, it can be isolating and excluding for employees who are legally obliged to stay away from colleagues and friends. Advice on how best to handle the process is offered by *GQ Magazine*, suggesting that the opportunity to take a step back and enjoy some downtime may be invaluable, and that, ultimately, the best thing to do might be to simply "Stop worrying and enjoy the cheques."[9]

Have you tried turning it off and on again?

A piece of advice offered in any situation where a device is not functioning as expected.

Now a routine suggestion for any situation where electronic devices seem to be unresponsive or have stopped working properly, *have you tried turning it off and on again?* became a common catchphrase after its regular usage in Channel 4's *The IT Crowd* (UK, 2006-2013). Created by Graham Linehan, the show revolved around the hapless members of an IT support department in a major corporation, with one member of the team, Roy, routinely asking any caller with an IT problem, *"Have you tried turning it off and on again?"* As the show evolves, Roy's increasing frustration is demonstrated by his use of the phrase before the caller has even had chance to say anything, by including it in an automated message to avoid having to even speak to the person raising the issue, and ultimately resorting to "have you tried sticking it up your arse"? Whilst the last of these is unlikely to solve many computer problems, any IT professional will confirm that *turning it off and on again* is indeed a good approach for the majority of issues that most users will experience with PCs, smartphones or any other gadgets they might own. Power cycling as a way to force a device to reinitialize is one of the first things to try to resolve any issue, as this provides an easy way to end any ongoing processes and start again, effectively decluttering the operating system and letting it start afresh. Whilst the suggestion is therefore not as flippant as it first sounds, it has still become a light-hearted response to anyone expressing annoyance at the unresponsiveness of their device (or, by extension, the non-responsiveness of anything at all).

Other suggestions from *The IT Crowd* as to how to deal with computer problems have been less successful in making it into wider circulation. Roy's colleague in the IT department, Moss, offers his own version of the same advice when he asks a caller, "Have You Tried Forcing an Unexpected Reboot?" Roy even resorts to more fundamental advice when he asks more than one caller, "Is it definitely plugged in?", subsequently discovering that this was indeed the problem. Similarly, attempts to introduce *The IT Crowd* to the wider world have been less than successful: a US version never made it beyond an unaired pilot, and a German version was cancelled after just two episodes, suggesting a particularly British affection for both the show itself, and the straightforward piece of advice that it spawned.

The prevalence of *have you tried turning it off and on again?* online demonstrates how widespread it has become. Extended examples of its use have cropped up in recent years, with one Twitter user responding to a power cut in London in August 2019 by asking whether it was "someone attempting to fix Britain by *turning it off and on again*".[10] The same idea was utilised in response to the US government shutdown in December 2018, showing that Internet users at least are happy to extend the metaphor to anything that seems like a good reboot might solve its problems.

Jump the shark

To go beyond the realms of credibility; the point at which something stretches plausibility to breaking point.

If ever a phrase was a good example of a modern idiom, *jump the shark* would be it. A fairly logical (but incorrect) assumption might be that *jumping the shark* describes something thrilling and breathtaking in the world of daredevil stunts. Instead, it describes the point at which a TV show or other entertainment franchise has more or less run out of ideas, and must resort to something ludicrous in order to try to bolster failing ratings or a decline in popularity. The idea has its origins in the TV show *Happy Days* (USA, 1974-1984), which followed the lives of the Cunningham family, in particular teenager Richie Cunningham and his friends, in 1950s and 60s middle America. By far the most memorable character was the iconic and unashamedly cool Arthur "Fonzie" Fonzarelli (otherwise known as "The Fonz"), who quickly grew from a peripheral figure in early episodes to a fan favourite and star of the show. At the start of series five of *Happy Days*, the gang travelled to Hollywood in a three-part episode, during which, amongst other things, The Fonz faced off against local loudmouth "The California Kid" in a water-skiing contest involving a jump over a caged tiger shark. Inevitably, our hero makes the jump and wins the day, but the fairly contrived nature of the incident gave rise to the phrase *jumping the shark* to mark the point at which a TV show stretches its credibility beyond breaking point. The reputation is a little undeserved given that *Happy Days* continued to run very successfully for a further six seasons (approximately 160 episodes) after this point, which doesn't exactly point to a fall into obscurity. *Happy Days* also provided the origin of alien "Mork" (Robin Williams), later of *Mork and Mindy* fame, so *jumping the shark* arguably doesn't even represent the most outlandish thing ever to appear on the show.

The phrase itself is said to have been first coined in 1985 by US radio personality Jon Hein and his then roommate Sean

Connolly, who at that time were both studying at the University of Michigan, during a conversation about worsening TV franchises. Hein went on to create website JumpTheShark.com, cataloguing shows that had suffered moments that marked an interminable decline, with over 200 examples. Modern usage is generally still applied to TV – in particular the much heralded final series of *Game of Thrones* was accused of multiple examples to prove it had done just that – but plenty of other things have also *jumped the shark* in recent years, with the term being applied in print to a whole host of entities considered to have stretched themselves beyond breaking point (see also *Nuke the fridge*, Chapter 3, for a comparable phrase in the world of movies).

One particularly productive domain seems to be the world of politics, and more specifically the response to the election of Donald Trump to the US Presidency in 2016. Even during his campaign, magazine editor Bill Kristol declared during a TV interview that Trump himself had *jumped the shark* with some of his pronouncements.[11] One writer in 2016 went further in response to Trump's apparent insinuation that Barack Obama and Hillary Clinton could be held responsible for founding ISIS, saying, "Trump hasn't *jumped the shark*. He's danced a jig on its head."[12] Going further still, Scottish comedian Frankie Boyle declared in 2017, "Now that Trump has been elected leader of the nominally free world, democracy has *jumped the shark*."[13] Comedy writer Armando Iannucci even declared in 2018 that he was leaving political satire to the younger generation, on the grounds that things had just gotten too unbelievable to lampoon, suggesting that, "The real world has *jumped the shark*."[14] Clearly no one saw 2020 coming.

Nudge nudge, wink wink
An indication that what is being said should be interpreted euphemistically.

Whilst not exactly a catchphrase (in the sense that it

wasn't a recurring theme), *nudge nudge, wink wink* is one of a plethora of well-known references from the absurd world of *Monty Python's Flying Circus* (UK, 1969-1974). Alongside such perennial favourites as "the dead parrot sketch", "The Ministry of Silly Walks" or "the lumberjack song", *nudge nudge, wink wink* sits as a classic piece of Pythonesque silliness. The sketch (officially entitled "Candid photography") appears in episode three of the first series, broadcast in the UK on BBC1 in October 1969. It features two of the Pythons: Terry Jones, who plays an unassuming and rather austere pub patron trying to enjoy a drink, and Eric Idle (who also wrote the sketch), as an excitable and overzealous gentleman who begins to bombard Jones with a series of barely disguised double-entendres, punctuated with phrases such as "know what I mean?", "*nudge nudge*" and "say no more". "*Wink wink*" is not particularly common in the original sketch, appearing only once, and then not in conjunction with "*nudge nudge*". Despite this, the phrase as a whole has become more broadly used to signify sexual innuendo, or simply to indicate that the speaker is being in some way euphemistic (and that she or he wants to make this fairly obvious). Macmillan Dictionary online lists an entry for *nudge nudge, wink wink*, defining it simply as "a way of saying indirectly that something involves sex".

Despite the widespread acclaim of *Monty Python* and its enduring popularity in British comedy culture, no other obvious examples have entered wider usage in the same way as *nudge nudge, wink wink*. As with other comedy catchphrases mentioned earlier in this chapter, the quotability of Python means that most people will know at least some of the hits (*Nobody expects the Spanish Inquisition, And now for something completely different* and *It's just a flesh wound* being three such examples). However, one particular sketch is notable for the sheer volume of idioms that it features. The aforementioned "dead parrot sketch" (also known as "The pet shop" sketch) features an exchange between a pet shop owner (Michael Palin) and an irate customer (John Cleese), who wishes to return a parrot on the grounds that it is (and was when it was purchased) stone dead. As the evasive Palin tries to claim that parrot is merely "resting", Cleese goes on to describe quite how dead the parrot is in a variety of ways ("it's expired and *gone to meet its maker*; if you hadn't nailed it to the perch it would be *pushing up the daisies*; it's *rung down the curtain* and *joined the choir invisible*"; the list goes on…) If nothing else, the sketch demonstrates quite how euphemistic we like to be when talking about the subject of death, with perhaps only one other topic coming close in terms of the number of innuendos we tend to use (if you know what I mean… *nudge nudge, wink wink*).

The 64,000 dollar question

A particularly important or difficult question or issue.

Sixty-four thousand dollars may not sound like a huge prize compared to some on offer in modern quiz shows, but in the 1950s it was substantially more valuable. An estimate based on the consumer price index and the average rate of inflation in the intervening time means that $64,000 in 1955 would be roughly equivalent to a little over $600,000 in 2020, which would represent a decent day's work by anyone's standards. The phrase can be used to describe an important or difficult question, hence a *64,000 dollar question* might be one that seems particularly puzzling, or which carries great significance. The amount comes from the TV quiz show of the same name (USA, 1955-1958), where contestants were asked to answer general knowledge questions on a specific chosen subject, with a cash prize that increased with each correct answer and a final question delivering a potential jackpot of $64,000. Despite huge initial success, growing competition from other shows and a major scandal involving the rigging of game shows in the USA during the 1950s led to a rather rapid fall from grace and subsequent cancellation. A revival of sorts came in 1976 with *The $128,000 Question*, with the increase in top prize prompted by the fact that rival quiz show *Name That Tune* had plans to add a top prize of $100,000.

Perhaps less well-known is the phrase *the 64 dollar question*, which was a precursor to *the 64,000 dollar question* in both linguistic and broadcasting terms. Sixty-four dollars was the top prize on the US radio quiz show *Take It or Leave It*, broadcast from 1940-1950 then under the name *The $64 Question* from 1950-1952. Several dictionaries, including Merriam-Webster online, list *the 64 dollar question* as the original idiom for a crucial or particularly challenging issue, even if nowadays such an amount might lead people to question just how challenging such a question could possibly be. *The 64,000 dollar question* is now less common than an equivalent like *the million dollar question*, although both are listed in various dictionaries with the same meaning (and a distinct increase in the use of *million dollar question* after the late 1990s suggests that we can attribute this directly to shows like *Who Wants to Be a Millionaire?* – see *Can I phone a friend?*, this chapter). Modern usage that is presumably derived from the original also extends to the *billion dollar question*, and even, in one article discussing the size of the US national debit in 2010, the *62 trillion dollar question*.[15]

Alternative uses might also apply to broader issues of great significance, where a *64,000 dollar question* (or derivatives) might relate to major challenges facing politicians or humanity more generally (how best to tackle climate change being an obvious example). Other uses tend to err more toward the ironic, highlighting the relative lack of importance of whatever is being asked. One example comes from a report on an interview between Prince Harry and Barack Obama in 2017, which describes the round of quick-fire questions that followed the more serious political conversation. Anglicising things a little, the report tells us that Harry probed Obama's TV preferences when he asked, "*the £64,000 question*: *Suits* or *The Good Wife*", suggesting both that the idiom is alive and well, and that it crosses the Atlantic with relatively little difficulty. (For those desperate to know, Obama chose *Suits*.)[16]

Something from the Twilight Zone
Something unusual, unexplained or seemingly supernatural.

Although a little on the old-fashioned side, most people would still recognise the description of odd or eerie events as being like *something from the Twilight Zone*. The original *Twilight Zone* was an anthology TV show that first aired in the USA from 1959-1964, with a run that featured around 150 episodes over five seasons. For many, even a rendition of the signature theme music would be enough to reference the show and imply that spooky goings on are very much on the cards. Created and presented by Rod Serling, the programme was a mix of science fiction, fantasy and horror, where ordinary people often found themselves in paranormal or other-worldly situations. Episodes usually ended with a twist of some kind, along with a moral, and often made some kind of social commentary. The who's who of actors, writers and directors involved in the show makes for impressive reading, with many household names cropping up in episodes before going on to bigger things. The iconic "Nightmare at 20,000 Feet", telling the story of an air traveller's terror at the hands of an aeroplane-destroying gremlin and starring a young William Shatner, is just one of the better-known examples, but other notable names (amongst many more) to appear along the way included film stars Robert Redford, Burt Reynolds, Robert Duvall and Charles Bronson; future *Columbo*, Peter Falk; stars of *Bewitched*, Elizabeth Montgomery and Dick York; and Shatner's fellow Star Trekkers, Leonard Nimoy and George Takei.

Revivals of the show in the 1980s, the early 2000s, and again in 2019, as well as movie and radio versions along the way, have meant that it remains in the public consciousness, and many episodes have popped up in pastiches, parodies and homages in a variety of settings. Notably, *The Simpsons* has made regular use of *The Twilight Zone* over the years, in particular in its Treehouse of Horror Halloween specials.[17] As well as multiple passing references (including at one point Homer commenting that a strange portal that he discovers behind a bookcase is "like something from that Twilighty show about that Zone"), more explicit parodies have included their own version of a vehicle destroying gremlin who terrorises Bart in "Terror at 5½ Feet", a take-off of *Twilight Zone* classic "To Serve Man" entitled "Hungry Are the Dammed" where the family are whisked away by aliens seemingly intent on eating them, and a parody of the *Twilight Zone* episode "Living Doll" entitled "Clown Without Pity" where Homer gifts Bart a talking doll that ends up trying to kill him. Rod Serling himself appears twice: once (voiced by Simpson regular Harry Shearer) to introduce the segment "Bart's Nightmare" (another *Twilight Zone* parody) in Treehouse of Horror II, and once in passing smoking a cigarette during the opening sequence of Treehouse of Horror XXIV. The list of cultural references appearing in *The Simpsons* makes it hard to say for certain, but *The Twilight Zone* must rank highly amongst the most borrowed from sources in its history.

The Free Dictionary, amongst other online sources, provides an alternative definition (still generally citing the TV show as the source) for *twilight zone* as an area of ambiguity, or the point where two states meet, hence people in legal limbo, or people crossing the boundary from friendship to romantic involvement, might be considered to be in the *twilight zone*. The first uses of *twilight zone* do pre-date the TV show by several decades, referring to both the eerie and less eerie senses of the idea. Reports of a debate on the "Extension of Tenure of Government Control of Railroads" stated the need to eliminate the "*twilight zone*" of mixed jurisdictions that existed at the time (1919). An article (also from 1919) entitled "In *the Twilight Zone*" discussed the "No Man's Land between the ground already conquered by science and the dark territory of mysticism, ignorance, and superstition."[18] Even earlier, a novel published in 1909 used the title *In the Twilight Zone*, suggesting that the term may well have been in circulation long before Rod Serling picked up the idea.

Starter for ten

An initial question or idea inviting further development.

A *starter for ten* is a starting point for discussion, or an initial question that will lead on to further questions or elaboration. The phrase comes from TV quiz *University Challenge* (UK, ITV: 1962-1987; BBC: 1994-present), which certainly sits amongst the more intellectually demanding of the many quiz shows that have appeared on our screens. Originally based on a US equivalent called *College Bowl*, the simplicity and unchanging nature of the show is often credited as one of the reasons for its longevity and ongoing appeal. The format has always been straightforward (at least compared to some quiz shows): two teams of four university students compete, with the highest scoring team being declared victorious. Initial questions – *starters for ten* – are worth ten points and must be answered individually on the buzzer, and a correct answer offers the team a further three questions worth five points each, which may be answered collectively. Current host Jeremy Paxman, in charge since the show's revival on the BBC in 1994, holds the distinction of being the longest running quiz host on British TV, adding to the sense of continuity. Given the often highly academic nature of questions posed on *University Challenge*, the meaning of a *starter for ten* as a relatively gentle initial question is perhaps a little misleading. An alternative, possibly more common use seems to be to introduce a topic, representing an initial idea for further discussion and elaboration.

Away from the questions and answers, *University Challenge*

provided the inspiration for a novel by David Nicholls in 2003, later adapted into a film in 2006. The story in both centres around Brian Jackson, a British university student in the mid-1980s, whose dream has always been to appear on the show. Although *Starter for Ten* provided the title of both novel and film in the UK, the relative obscurity of the phrase elsewhere meant that the book was released under the alternative title *A Question of Attraction* in the USA (although the filmmakers felt no need to also adopt an alternative title). Elsewhere, 1980s British TV comedy *The Young Ones* paid merciless homage to *University Challenge* in the first episode of its second series, entitled "Bambi" (a reference to original presenter, Bamber Gascoigne). The cast – a set of students at the fictional "Scumbag College" – take on a team from the equally fictional "Footlights College, Oxbridge", incurring the wrath of the crowd by tampering with the questions, accidentally urinating on their opponents (the multilevel nature of the two teams being another aspect of the parody), and finally blowing the opposition up with a grenade.

In real life, victory on *University Challenge* has come with mixed success in other walks of life. A documentary broadcast in 2009 reported on the struggles of some previous winners, and a *Telegraph* article on the subject asked its own *starter for ten*, pondering why so many of its "impossibly bright contestants" went on to lead underachieving or even troubled lives.[19] Happily, there are plenty of success stories too, and in recent years "Human Google" Gail Trimble (captain of the Corpus Christi College, Oxford team in 2009) and, more recently, Eric Monkman (captain of Wolfson College, Cambridge in 2017) became minor celebrities following their highly successful appearances on the show. In the case of Monkman, an unlikely broadcasting career followed (along with fellow *University Challenge* contestant Bobby Seagull), as well as adoration from his fans in the form of the hashtag #Monkmania, coined during his side's run to the final, and even an online store selling T-shirts with his face on them. It's presumably not exactly what people go to Cambridge University for, but nice to hear the kind of fame and fortune that can result simply from having an "expressive face".[20]

Ten four

An indication that a message has been received and understood.

An example of a phrase popularised by, rather than originating from, a TV show, *ten four* survives as one of the only examples of a set of radio codes by the Association of Public-Safety Communications Officials-International (APCO) as a way of abbreviating radio transmissions. Charles Hopper of the Illinois State Police is generally credited with the invention of Ten Signals in 1937, largely because of a common problem with early radio which meant that the initial syllables of transmissions were often not heard (since the way radios were powered meant that they took a fraction of a second to warm up). By developing a list of codes, each preceded with "ten", the important element (the second number) would not be lost, which also allowed for brevity in communication at a time when bandwidth was more limited.

The codes were popularised to a television audience by the US TV series *Highway Patrol* (USA, 1955-1959), which ran for four series during the latter part of the 1950s. The show was a police drama/action series set in an unidentified state in the Western USA, and officers (chiefly star of the show Broderick Crawford, who played police chief Dan Mathews) would regularly use ten codes as part of their communication. *Ten four* – meaning "message received", "affirmative" or simply "OK" – became synonymous with the show, and later reruns even aired under this name. The full list of Ten codes underwent plenty of development over the years, and have largely been superseded in modern communications with everyday language equivalents, but one other to survive more or less into modern vocabulary is code ten twenty, meaning "What is your location?", itself often abbreviated in phrases like *what's your twenty?*

One reason for the continuation of such phrases is their regular inclusion in police and trucker movies or TV shows over the years, as well as the explosion of interest in the Citizens Band (or CB) radio during the 1970s. Movies like *Smokey and the Bandit* (the second highest grossing movie of 1977, second only to the original *Star Wars*), *Breaker! Breaker!* (released a few months prior to *Smokey and the Bandit*, but markedly less of a commercial success) and *Convoy* (1978) all capitalised on the interest in CB radio communications and the trucking industry in general toward the end of the 1970s. Richard Ramsey, writing in *The Journal of Popular Culture* in 1979, suggested that the widespread popularity of CB radio rivalled other inventions such as the television or telephone in terms of its technological and cultural impact on American life.[21] With 40 years' hindsight, this feels like a claim that has not entirely stood the test of time, but multiple lists of CB slang are freely available online that suggest interest is still as strong as ever in the right circles.

Trigger's broom

Something that is claimed to be the same despite extensive modifications.

Trigger's broom is a modern version of a philosophical thought experiment, most commonly referred to as "the ship of Theseus". The original is based on the story of Theseus who, amongst other heroic feats in ancient Greek legend, was known for fighting and slaying the Minotaur on the island of Crete. On his return, the ship he sailed home in was honoured and preserved in Athens harbour. Over time, as the wooden planks that made up the ship began to rot, they were removed and replaced, so as to retain the integrity of the ship as a whole. The question that arises, according to the many philosophers who have considered it over the years, is whether the entire vessel could be replaced piece by piece and still be considered to be the same ship at the end. The puzzle poses intriguing questions about the nature of being, and how much something can change before it is no longer still the same original thing.

The modern equivalent comes from TV sitcom *Only Fools and Horses* (UK, 1981-2003), which ran for over 20 years between the early 1980s and early 2000s. The Trigger in question was a simple-minded character who worked as a road sweeper for his local council. In an episode screened as part of the Christmas trilogy in 1996 entitled "Heroes and Villains", Trigger is given an award for having saved the council money by using the same broom in his job for the past 20 years. When asked how this is possible, he suggests that he has looked after his broom well, and that it had only had "17 new heads and 14 new handles in its time". When asked how it could therefore be the same broom, Trigger responds by showing a photo of him holding the broom, asking what more proof could possibly be needed.

Although *Trigger's broom* is not the most widespread of the modern idioms considered here, it does still crop up enough to suggest that it has entered the vocabulary for at least some people. Examples found online often relate to the restoration of things like classic cars, watches, computers, rifles and bikes, all of which, it is suggested, face the same dilemma of "sameness" once most or all of the original components have been replaced over time. Some classic rock bands also seem to be appropriately described in such terms, with multiple examples of groups losing almost entire line-ups but still soldiering on for years to come.[22]

As one of the most beloved sitcoms in British TV history, *Only Fools and Horses* is another example (like *Monty Python's Flying Circus*, *Fawlty Towers* or *Dad's Army*) where we can identify plenty of catchphrases and lines that have made their way into the language. A 2015 survey by UK TV channel Gold revealed *lovely jubbly* as the most enduring of main character Del Boy's catchphrases, alongside other favourites such as the perennially English insult *you plonker*, and the use of *cushti* (or *cushty*, *kushti* or *cushdy*, depending on your spelling preference) to mean "good".[23] This last example is thought to have made its way into Cockney from Romani, but Del Boy is certainly credited with introducing it to a much wider audience (in the UK, at least).

In the spirit of 1990s shock-fest *The Jerry Springer Show*, it seems appropriate to offer a "final thought" to round things off. TV has contributed so much to modern life, and as well as the idioms considered here, we might also add words like *d'oh!* or *meh* (The Simpsons) and *bazinga* (The Big Bang Theory) to our repertoire, along with many, many more. We can even go beyond the realms of UK and US television to unearth other examples of TV-inspired phrases. Australians adopted the phrase *Not happy, Jan!* following its use in a Yellow Pages advert in 2000, as a way of expressing annoyance at someone else's incompetence.[24] Not exactly an idiom but sure to be more widely known outside of Australia, another stereotypical phrase – *shrimp on the barbie* – can also be traced to a TV advert, this time aimed at US audiences, which featured a (pre-Crocodile Dundee) Paul Hogan encouraging tourists to visit Australia. In the advert Hogan offered to *slip another shrimp on the barbie*, and the phrase took root as a general reference to Australian culture the world over (albeit not necessarily one that many Australians particularly like).[25]

Who knows whether changing viewing habits in the 21st century will stem the flow of TV-inspired idioms. To find out, maybe we'll just need to keep on watching.

3

Silver Tongues and Silver Screens: Idioms from the Movies

In 2005 the American Film Institute charged a panel of industry professionals with the task of compiling the 100 most memorable film quotations of the past 100 years. Jean Picker Firstenberg, CEO of the AFI at the time that the list was published, explained, "Great movie quotes become part of our cultural vocabulary", and certainly most people will feature at least some iconic soundbites or pithy one-liners in their linguistic repertoires.[1] An updated list by the *Hollywood Reporter* in 2016 shows a considerable amount of overlap, with Clark Gable's *Frankly, my dear, I don't give a damn* (Gone with the Wind, 1939) topping both lists. Universally recognised as it is, it is difficult to make a case for this as an idiom, but plenty of other memorable lines are at least borderline cases. Examples might include *I've a feeling we're not in Kansas anymore* (The Wizard of Oz, 1939), widely adopted throughout TV history to indicate that characters have turned up in an unknown or unexpected location; *Houston, we have a problem* (Apollo 13, 1995), indicating that an unforeseen issue has cropped up and needs to be dealt with; and *Life is like a box of chocolates* (Forrest Gump, 1994), used as perhaps the best known metaphor (or, technically speaking, simile) for life being full of surprises where "you never know what you're gonna get". Other movies have become such an established part of public consciousness that it's easy to forget their contribution to the language. No one had heard of lightsabers, Jedi mind tricks or The Force prior to *Star Wars* being released in 1977, but all are now firmly embedded in the lexicon.

Just as for TV in the previous chapter, the examples included in this section include quotations, taglines or even titles that have grown beyond their original use and now exist as phrases in their own right. In some cases the origins are surprising, but all represent examples of life imitating art, at least in a linguistic sense.

All singing, all dancing

Something that features an array of impressive features.

The Broadway Melody (1929; also known as *The Broadway Melody of 1929*, to distinguish it from sequels with the same name in 1936, 1938 and 1940) was fairly revolutionary at a time when cinema was dominated by both a lack of dialogue and a lack of colour. As well as being one of the first musical films to feature a technicolour sequence, it was also the first sound film to win an Oscar for Best Picture, which it did at the second Academy Awards ceremony in 1930, honouring films released between 1st August 1928 and 31st July 1929. It also spawned the idiom *all singing, all dancing*, which appeared on the promotional poster, actually as part of the slightly longer "All talking, *all singing, all dancing*", to highlight the vivacity and vigour that audiences could expect.

Uses of the phrase now seem to cluster into two main groups. One is more or less a factual description, applied to musicals, films, shows, or other spectaculars where there is, literally, lots of singing and dancing going on. In the second, more idiomatic sense, things that are *all singing, all dancing* generally come with a host of features, but often this designation comes with an implication that this is not necessarily a good thing. Multiple references online to things like computer software, photocopiers and other modern-world essentials decry the introduction of *all singing, all dancing* innovations that may end up being more trouble than they are worth. Similarly, residents of the UK town of Malton in North Yorkshire objected vehemently to proposed plans for "an *all singing all dancing* superstore which risks bankrupting existing local traders", highlighting the opposition that can often accompany such developments.[2] A distinctly more dystopian use of the phrase crops up in 1999 movie *Fight Club* (having previously appeared in the 1996 novel of the same name by Chuck Palahniuk), when main character Tyler Durden sums up the frustration of modern life by describing his followers as "the *all singing all dancing* crap of the world." It seems like a far cry from the music halls of the 1920s, but it didn't stop him from making his point.

All singing, all dancing now appears as an entry in multiple online dictionaries, and the move from a literal description of musical theatre to a more abstract comment on the array of features on show seems to have happened sometime toward the end of the 1970s. References in Google Books up until 1978 seem to exclusively use the phrase in reference to stage and screen, but by 1980 we get a use relating to developments in the fairly niche context of cartographical technology. An article on "The Changing Scene in Surveying and Mapping" from December 1980 talks about the new "*all-singing, all-dancing*" National Digital Cartographic Data Base, launched in the USA as part of the National Mapping Program at the start of the 1980s. From the middle of that decade, as technology began to take off in a huge range of areas, so did the use of *all singing, all dancing* as a (not always overly positive) way to describe the great leap forward.

Bucket list

A list of things to accomplish before dying.

Derived from a more established idiom, a *bucket list* is a list of things to do before you die, or more colloquially, before you *kick the bucket*. Although the idea of *kicking the bucket* has been around in English for centuries (see Chapter 1), *bucket list* seems to have emerged principally as a result of the 2007 film of the same name, featuring Jack Nicholson and Morgan Freeman as terminal cancer patients who decide to spend the final months of their lives attempting to cross as many things as possible off their own lists. Multiple sources credit screenwriter Justin Zackham with coining the phrase, and the first recorded uses in the wider world were in articles about the upcoming film from June 2006. Zackham apparently came up with his own "List of Things to Do Before I *Kick the Bucket*" (later shortened to "Justin's *Bucket List*") when he first moved to LA to pursue a career in film. Top of the list was to have a movie made by a major Hollywood studio, and he used the list as inspiration to write a script with the working title of *The Bucket List*. The script eventually found its way to director Rob Reiner, who thought the idea, and title, were worth pursuing.[3]

People took the idea and the phrase to heart and in 2012 *bucket list* was added to multiple dictionaries. A search for *bucket list* now returns a wealth of suggestions from lifestyle websites for how people might populate their own, as well as directing people toward various goal-setting platforms that help members to keep track of their various objectives. It even leads to the example of the *"bucket list* family", Garrett and Jessica Gee, who sold everything they had in 2015 and decided to spend their time travelling the world with their two young children. Three years later (and having added a third child along the way) they had visited 65 different countries, documenting their journey along the way as travel journalists.[4] On the other side of the debate, some critics have suggested that rather than making aspirational lists (that likely contain many of the same things as everyone else's list would), people should concentrate on living life in the moment, enjoying the connections that we can build with other human beings. Psychotherapist Philippa Perry even joked that *bucket lists* may have been started as PR stunts by companies involved in selling life-affirming experiences such as swimming with dolphins, and decried the commercial and individualistic nature of the whole endeavour.[5]

Such objections haven't stopped the *bucket list* becoming

firmly rooted in public consciousness, and several TV shows have also tapped into the notion. UK TV show *An Idiot Abroad* saw broadcaster Karl Pilkington travelling the world, with the second series – "the *Bucket List*" – in 2011 focusing on activities including bungee jumping, travelling on the Trans-Siberian railway and driving Route 66 in an open-top Cadillac. A 2017 BBC sitcom entitled *Bucket* (tagline: "Watch it before you kick it") featured a mother and daughter on a road trip aiming to tick things off the mother's fairly extravagant list, including the ambition to streak at a major sporting event (dog show Crufts is chosen as a suitable candidate). Will Smith also launched his own *Bucket List* TV show, screened on the Facebook Watch video-on-demand service, where he marked turning 50 by tackling his own personal list of ambitions, including skydiving, dune buggy racing in the desert and trying his hand at stand-up comedy. But a *bucket list* of a very different type is offered in sitcom *Moone Boy*, created by Irish actor and comedian Chris O'Dowd (better known as Roy in *The IT Crowd*; see *Have you tried turning it off and on again?*, Chapter 2), which ran on Sky TV in the UK from 2012 to 2015. In the final episode of season three, entitled "Gershwin's *Bucket List*", the show's main character, 12-year-old Martin Moone, is discussing *bucket lists* with his imaginary friend, Sean Murphy (played by O'Dowd). Sean Murphy seems surprised that Martin would have a *bucket list* at such a young age, but Martin replies that his is simply a list of things that he keeps inside a red plastic bucket. His list includes a towel, a trowel, a pair of driving gloves and, appropriately, a list of things he wants to do before he dies.

Bunny boiler

An unpredictable and potentially dangerous romantic partner.

Bunny boiler is indirectly attributed to the 1987 movie *Fatal Attraction*, a psychological thriller starring Glenn Close and Michael Douglas. The movie tells the story of a married man

(Douglas) who has a short-lived extramarital fling. The jilted woman (Close), however, refuses to allow the affair to end, becoming increasingly desperate and unhinged in her attempts to cling on to the relationship. The fateful scene comes after Close has already demonstrated plenty of evidence that she may not be too willing to let the relationship go without a fight. Douglas has long since broken off the affair and his wife, unaware of what has transpired previously, returns home to find an ominously bubbling pot on the stove. Upon investigating, and at the same time as we see in a parallel scene that the family's pet rabbit is missing from its cage, she finds that the poor bunny has been killed and left to boil in a pot of water.

The term *bunny boiler* itself is conspicuous in its absence from the film, emerging some time later and retrospectively applied to the character. Some sources attribute its coinage to Glenn Close herself, and the first record of the term being used in print comes from December 1990, in the *Dallas Morning News* (itself reporting an interview Close gave to the *Ladies' Home Journal*), where Close said, "There's nothing like portraying a psychopathic *bunny boiler* to boost one's self-esteem." The Phrase Finder website suggests that it was not until 1994 that *bunny boiler* began showing signs of regular use, and the term is now fairly liberally applied in a range of contexts. These have included the contestants on TV show *The Bachelor* (contestants in 2012 were apparently "even crazier than last year's *bunny boilers*"), several references to the women of soap operas (including Joan Collins as Alexis Carrington in *Dynasty*, described as a *"bunny boiler"* and one of "four top TV bitches" by a reviewer in 2010),[6] and in one article in *The Spectator*, even to Princess Diana's *"Bunny Boiler"* Years".[7] We also get a rather disturbing real-life example (not of *bunny boiling* but not a million miles away) from a news article in early 2019, where a Louisiana man was accused of having eaten an ex-girlfriend's pet fish several years previously. Subsequently charged with animal cruelty (and with evading justice, having failed to respond to the original summons over the incident), one reader of the story commented that the man in question was clearly a "straight up *bunny boiler* type", suggesting that the term can be applied just as appropriately to men as to women.

More extended examples include the Italian football team AS Roma, whose fans can apparently be "real *bunny boilers* if they aren't happy with your performance".[8] This may represent a touch of journalistic licence, coming as it did in a report about Roma fans protesting a string of poor performances, in which the players had played like "rabbits", by delivering a large quantity of carrots to the team. Another usage comes in an article describing the toxic influence of misinformation on the vote by the UK to leave the EU in 2016.[9] This piece described how another journalist had happily spread the entirely untrue story that EU directives would force people to boil dead pets in a pressure cooker for half an hour prior to burying them. Such scaremongering apparently meant that readers were only too happy to "leave behind the EU's *bunny boilers*". In the interests of accuracy, the story was easily and thankfully debunked on the Euromyths section of the European Commission website, which described it rather straightforwardly as "rubbish".

Difficult difficult, lemon difficult

An indication that a problem is not at all straightforward (the opposite of easy peasy, lemon squeezy).

A phrase that has developed into a meme in its own right (see Chapter 4 for more on memes), *difficult difficult, lemon difficult* was first coined in 2009 satirical movie *In the Loop*, which features members of the UK and US governments trying to deal with an escalating military situation in the Middle East. The phrase *difficult difficult, lemon difficult* is first uttered by political aide Toby Wright, in response to a suggestion by his boss, Minister for International Development Simon Foster, that he should try to "pump" a member of the US State Department for information. Foster states that it should be "easy peasy, lemon squeezy", to which Toby replies, "No it won't. It'll be *difficult difficult, lemon difficult*." Foster subsequently repeats the phrase (to very bemused looks) during a meeting to decide whether the joint forces should press on with an invasion of the Middle East, saying, "In my country, we have a great saying for situations such as this, which is: It's *difficult, difficult, lemon difficult*."

Co-writer of the film Simon Blackwell is quoted as saying that he came up with the line in his garden one day and decided to include it, confident that one of the writing team would veto it if it didn't work.[10] The phrase stayed in, and joined another memorable coinage from the TV show that had been the basis for the movie. *In the Loop* was a movie spin-off of BBC TV comedy *The Thick of It*, and both offerings satirised the inner workings of government (*The Thick of It* just concerned the UK; *In the Loop* took aim at both the UK and US administrations), often portraying flustered politicians as they try to respond to and contain potentially damaging situations. *The Thick of It* introduced foul-mouthed spin doctor Malcolm Tucker, who memorably described one minister as an "omnishambles" in response to a series of exasperating embarrassments. Omnishambles – meaning a situation that is shambolic in every conceivable way – quickly gained in popularity, being crowned the Oxford English Dictionary's word of the year for 2012, and formally entering the lexicon in 2013.

Difficult difficult, lemon difficult has also developed a life beyond its original usage. A series of *difficult difficult, lemon difficult* memes can be found online, where you can also buy T-shirts, cushions, mugs and even baby clothes bearing the message. Urban Dictionary lists *difficult difficult, lemon difficult* as "the awkwardly worded antonym to 'Easy peasy, lemon squeezy'", itself a phrase that seems to have a surprisingly modern origin. Word Histories lists a first recorded usage in

1983,[11] although according to Dictionary.com, the shorter "easy peasy" goes back at least another few decades, appearing in 1940 US movie *The Long Voyage Home*.[12] Some sources attribute the "lemon squeezy" part to a brand of (lemon-scented) washing-up liquid called Squezy, launched in the UK in the 1950s. Although this may well have contributed to the development of the phrase, its slogan – "It's easy with Squezy", first used in 1957 – didn't mention lemons, so any association may be purely accidental.

Groundhog Day

An event that seems to recur over and over again, or which seems depressingly familiar and predictable.

Groundhog Day has become synonymous with a feeling of déjà vu, thanks to the film of the same name released in 1993. The movie stars Bill Murray as an arrogant and acerbic weatherman – Phil Connors – who finds himself stranded in the small town of Punxsutawney, Pennsylvania following a freak snowstorm. On waking the next day, he finds himself stuck in a time-loop, and subsequently lives through the same day over and over. The film charts his progress through bafflement, disbelief, anger, despair, and eventually enlightenment, as he gradually learns to embrace the experience and live a more selfless, kinder life. *Groundhog Day* has subsequently come to describe any recurrent situation where time seems to be repeating itself, especially in a way that feels depressingly predictable or inevitable.

The phrase was reported to be in use by the American military soon after the film's release: one early use appeared in an article from September 1993 about the monotony of life aboard aircraft carrier the *USS America*. Multiple uses have been recorded since (including by President Bill Clinton in 1996), and an article on military slang from 2007 includes *Groundhog Day* with the meaning "Every day of your tour in Iraq".[13] Evidence of its widespread adoption comes from the fact that by 2012 it was being decried as a journalistic cliché, "leached almost entirely of its meaning" by its overuse, amongst, in particular, sports journalists and political reporters.[14] Such pessimism has not prevented its continued usage, for example in 2018 when one journalist commented on Trump's perceived more presidential demeanour at the funeral of George Bush (merely for having sat through it without causing a scene). Since it was quickly back to business as usual, the writer lamented, "Alas, it was another *Groundhog Day* in a loop of Trumpian false dawns."[15] In the UK, Prime Minister Boris Johnson promised to "end the *groundhoggery* of Brexit" during the UK general election campaign in 2019.[16] The phrase is now fully established in English, with most dictionaries listing both the day itself (February 2nd – by tradition the day in many parts of North America when a local groundhog predicts whether spring is ready to arrive or whether winter will continue for six more weeks) and the more idiomatic meaning amongst its definitions.

Groundhog Day is also the main source of comparison for any movie or TV show that employs the time-loop as a plot device. The first example in fiction may be the short story *Doubled and Redoubled* by Malcolm Jameson, published in 1941. Another short story, *12.01 P.M.* by Richard A. Lupoff, published in 1973, also centred around a time-loop and was subsequently made into both a short film (in 1990) and a TV movie (in 1993). Despite these forerunners, TV Tropes lists the "'*Groundhog Day*' loop" as any plot utilising this idea, noting that it is probably the example that established the time-loop in mainstream pop culture. As further proof of its enduring appeal, *Groundhog Day* even inspired a stage musical adaption in 2016. Bill Murray attended, and by all accounts thoroughly enjoyed, the Broadway staging of the show in August 2017. What did he do the next night? He went again, of course.[17]

Know where the bodies are buried

To have knowledge of the unpleasant secrets of a person or organisation.

Orson Welles' 1941 movie *Citizen Kane* regularly appears on lists of the best films that Hollywood has produced. It is generally praised for its cinematography, direction and bravura performance by Welles himself in the title role. The script (written by Welles in collaboration with Herman Mankiewicz) won an Academy Award for Best Original Screenplay. It is also the likely, if little recognised, source of the phrase *know where the bodies are buried*, meaning to have inside knowledge of distinctly questionable (if not outright illegal) actions, especially in political or business terms. The origin of the phrase makes perfect sense in the context of the movie, which relates the life and times of the fictional newspaper magnate Charles Foster Kane, in particular charting the efforts of reporter Jerry Thompson to uncover the meaning of Kane's dying word: "Rosebud". Thompson sets about interviewing a range of Kane's friends, family and associates, including Susan Alexander, Kane's second wife. Her advice is to "talk to Raymond" (Kane's butler), since "He *knows where the bodies are buried*", indicating that this was where the really juicy details of Kane's life and business operations could be found.

Both the Oxford English Dictionary and The Phrase Finder website cite *Citizen Kane* as the first usage, but an interesting take on this comes from an article from June 2015, which suggests that although the phrase itself originates from the film, its inclusion might be based on an earlier draft of the screenplay that featured actual buried bodies as part of the shady goings on in Charles Foster Kane's life.[18] Although we can't be sure of the accuracy of the claim (the writer of the article points out that it came from a piece by a *New Yorker* film critic whose motives have been questioned), it would make sense as a way to extend the meaning to encompass both literal and metaphorical "bodies". Nowadays the phrase is commonly used in its metaphorical form, with reference to people who may have intimate knowledge that might, in some instances, grant them a certain amount of leverage. One example would be the case of Michael Flynn, at one time National Security advisor to Donald Trump, who resigned in February 2017 amidst a scandal over possible Russian interference in the 2016 US election. An article published a month following his resignation suggested that Flynn's attempt to gain immunity might have been something of a bluff, since Flynn may or may not *"know where the bodies are buried*, if there were bodies to be found".[19]

The Word Histories website lists some earlier instances of the phrase, suggesting that *Citizen Kane* may not be the clear source that others have suggested it is.[20] The earliest, from 1928, comes from a single paragraph in a Louisiana newspaper, stating (about an unidentified subject), "something needs to be done to supress this chap. He knows too much about us. *He knows where the body is buried.*" The lack of further context and the use of "body" (singular) makes it difficult to say whether this is literal or not, but the sense of the phrase is certainly apparent even in this short extract. Another use, again with the singular "body", appears in a newspaper column from 1930, referring to a seemingly untouchable Republican chairman. By 1931, an article on the "blackmail racket" in the American film industry highlighted the backstabbing and cutthroat nature of Hollywood at the time, when "every one [was] trying to get something over on the other fellow". The article went on to comment, "You see some obvious incompetent hoisted into a job away [sic] over his head and immediately the whisper goes round, 'he *knows where the bodies are buried*'." Whilst Orson Welles might therefore not exactly have coined the phrase himself, perhaps his experience in the movie industry at the time certainly helped to suggest it as a particularly appropriate way to express the sentiment he was looking for.

Nuke the fridge

The point at which a film demonstrates itself to be of inferior quality to previous instalments.

Fans waited almost 20 years for a fourth instalment of the Indiana Jones film franchise and it's fair to say that reaction following the release of *Indiana Jones and the Kingdom of the Crystal Skull* in 2008 was mixed. One particular point of disgruntlement stemmed from the opening action scene, when, having infiltrated a secret warehouse in the Nevada desert, Indiana Jones escapes from the Soviet agents who have captured him and takes refuge in a model town, quickly realising it to be a test site for the firing of an atomic bomb. With seconds to spare he shelters inside a lead-lined refrigerator, which is catapulted some distance away by the blast, leaving Indy to emerge entirely unscathed. Fans were so outraged at the over the top and implausible nature of the scene that they quickly took to message boards to bemoan the fact, and various sources have reported that *nuke the fridge* was already in usage a mere two days after the release of the film. According to Know Your Meme, the first entry appeared on Urban Dictionary on 26th May 2008, defined as the moment where, "it becomes apparent that a certain instalment is not as good as previous instalments, due to ridiculous or low quality storylines, events or characters."[21]

Users quickly made parallels to the more established and widespread *jump the shark* (see Chapter 2), used to describe TV shows that have similarly gone downhill and pushed their storylines beyond all credibility. The review website Slash Film even published an article in 2008 asking whether *nuke the fridge* was the new *jump the shark*,[22] but ten years later on it shows no signs of really making it beyond the (relatively niche) world of Internet message boards and movie criticism. Most search results for the phrase discuss it in terms of the incident itself, often focusing on two major points of discussion. The first concerns the plausibility of the whole thing, with opinion split as to how scientifically accurate Indy's survival might have been. George Lucas had apparently put together his own research, estimating that the chances of survival were around 50-50, but a rather tongue-in-cheek attempt at peer review by the scientific community put the odds a lot closer to zero.[23] An alternative analysis came to the exact opposite conclusion, deciding that almost all aspects of the set-piece were plausible,[24] and multiple other sources exist online to take up the question in a very earnest fashion, if nothing else proving that a lot of people have too much time on their hands.

The second point of debate is whether *nuking the fridge* even represents the most outlandish thing to happen during an Indiana Jones movie, with plenty of other candidates for moments that require an equally large suspension of disbelief. In 2016, culture website Inverse listed six moments that it considered to be more ridiculous throughout the Indiana Jones franchise (including the presence of a 700-year-old knight guarding the Holy Grail in *Indiana Jones and the Last Crusade*).[25] In 2014, movie review website Film School Rejects ran a similar comparison, concluding that, alongside other implausible situations throughout the franchise, *nuking the fridge* was simply "par for the course".[26] Despite the generally negative response to the scene itself, director Steven Spielberg clearly was not too concerned with the criticism, even expressing his pride in the new phrase that he had spawned when he said: "People stopped saying *'jump the shark'*. They now say, *'nuked the fridge'*. I'm proud of that. I'm glad I was able to bring that into popular culture."[27]

Sleep with the fishes

To be dead, specifically killed and buried in water.

Based on the 1969 novel of the same name by Mario Puzo (who also co-wrote the screenplay for the subsequent movie), 1972's *The Godfather* has many claims to fame. For four years after its release it held the title of highest grossing film ever made (*Jaws* overtook this mark in 1976). It is credited with reviving the career of Marlon Brando, launching the careers of, amongst others, Al Pacino and director Francis Ford Coppola, and ranks second on the American Film Institute's list of 100 greatest American movies of all time released in 2007. The phrase *sleep with the fishes* appears midway through, when Don Corleone (Brando), the titular Godfather of the Corleone crime family, sends his personal enforcer, Luca Brasi, to meet with rival gangsters. They strangle Brasi, and subsequently send back his bullet-proof vest filled with fish, which is explained as "a Sicilian message. It means Luca Brasi *sleeps with the fishes*." The same idea (but not the phrase itself) appeared in the original novel, where it was explained that the fish signified that Brasi was "sleeping on the bottom of the ocean".

Some evidence suggests that the phrase pre-dates this example (although *The Godfather* certainly helped to popularise it), and may not be restricted to the Sicilian Mafia at all. A 2011 article on the Grammarphobia blog suggests that it was in use as early as the 1830s, when British Travel Writer Captain Edmund Spencer described the very hostile reaction encountered by a fly fisherman on a visit to a small town in Germany.[28] The locals considered him to be practising a form of black magic and, having "forcibly put to flight the magician himself", the superstitious German villagers allegedly threatened that "if he repeated his visit, they would send him to *sleep with the fishes*".

Nowadays the phrase has evolved into a more general euphemism for "dead", even if most uses do centre around a watery grave of some kind, or make allusions to criminal activity. However, *The Simpsons* included a novel take on the idea in a 1996 episode entitled "A Fish Called Selma". The episode centres on fading movie star Troy McClure, with several characters making suggestive comments throughout that he had been involved in some kind of "scandal" at an aquarium. In one scene, when gangsters Louie and Fat Tony spot McClure, Louie says to his boss, "Hey, I thought you said Troy McClure was dead?" Fat Tony, head of the Springfield Mafia, replies, "No, what I said was 'He *sleeps with the fishes'*...", but is (fortunately) cut off before he can elaborate on the full nature of McClure's activities.

One other phrase popularised by *The Godfather* is also worth considering here. Perhaps the most memorable line in the film – second on the AFI list of greatest quotations – is *I'm gonna make him an offer he can't refuse*. In the movie (and original novel), the line is uttered by Don Corleone as a veiled threat, implying that the "offer" will be to do what he says or else face the consequences. The Phrase Finder suggests that this was already in common usage, citing an example from 1934 film *Burn 'Em Up Barnes* where the meaning was more straightforward: the offer would be so lucrative that the person in question would be unable to turn it down. In the case of *The Godfather*, the "offer" is accompanied by the severed head of the recipient's racehorse, which, unsurprisingly, leads to the message being heard loud and clear. Modern usage (since most people don't tend to resort to such measures) tends to be of the more generous variety.

Finally, a line from *The Godfather: Part II* (1974) is often misattributed to much earlier sources. In *Part II*, Michael Corleone (played by Al Pacino), having taken over as the new head of the family, tells one of his associates that his father taught him to *"keep your friends close but your enemies closer."* The line (number 58 on the AFI memorable quotations list) is sometimes assumed to be an old proverb, associated with, amongst others, Chinese general and author of *The Art of War*, Sun Tzu, or Italian writer and philosopher, Niccolò Machiavelli. Although in *The Prince*, Machiavelli did allude to the idea of paying more attention to enemies than friends as a way of winning them to your cause, all evidence points to *The Godfather: Part II* as the first time this particular phrase was used. The implication (at least in Mafia terms) is not just that it is useful to have close knowledge of what your enemies might be up to, but also that it may be prudent to try to prevent them from realising that they are even your enemies at all. In more optimistic terms, various sources have used the phrase to comment on the prudence of cooperation rather than hostility between business rivals, or simply to point out that keeping some of the worst experiences we have as silent reminders may be the best way to realise how far we've come in life.

Sliding doors moment

A pivotal moment where a different decision could lead to an entirely different course of events.

Sliding Doors was a 1998 romantic comedy that deserves acclaim if only for the originality of its premise. Gwyneth Paltrow plays Helen, who at the start of the film is fired from her job at a PR firm. As she runs to catch the train home on the London Underground, the story suddenly diverges and we are offered two versions. In one, she boards the train, arriving home in time to catch her boyfriend in bed with another woman, causing her to leave him and move on with her life in a variety of positive ways. In the second version she misses the train, and as a result arrives home too late to catch her partner in the act, precipitating an entirely different path. The phrase *sliding doors moment* entered the vocabulary shortly after the film was released to describe pivotal moments that have the potential to drastically alter the course of future events. A similar idea (also used as the premise and title of a movie but originating from the work of mathematician and meteorologist Edward Lorenz) is *The Butterfly Effect*, where small changes at one point in time (such as a butterfly flapping its wings) can have unpredictably larger effects in the future.

Twenty years on from the film's release, writer and director Peter Howitt reflected on his own *sliding doors moment*, when he was almost hit by a car following a split second decision to dash across the road to make a phone call. He even related his excitement at hearing Ringo Starr use the phrase to describe his own pivotal moment: defying his parents by going to play drums rather than becoming an electrician.[29] The idea of a *sliding doors moment* is now firmly established in popular culture, and Wikipedia even lists an entirely non-exhaustive and largely speculative list of modern examples, headed by Princess Diana's last minute decision to cut short her holiday in the Mediterranean and spend a night in Paris on her way home to London in 1997. A 2018 article on an Australian news website claimed that Diana's life was dominated by such *sliding doors moments*.[30] A *Guardian* article in 2019 presented six sporting *sliding doors* moments, ranging in severity from a turned ankle for Australian fast bowler Glenn McGrath (which may or may not have helped England regain the Ashes in 2005), to the decision by the Football Association in 1921 to ban women's football in the UK (on the grounds that it was threatening the men's game and "ought not to be encouraged").[31] Elsewhere, multiple sources reflect on the concept of the *sliding doors moment*, suggesting that it is firmly embedded in the public consciousness.

To mark the launch of its digital travel update service in 2019, London North Eastern Railway conducted a survey that discovered around 80% of the British public claim to have experienced a *sliding doors moment* at some point in their lives.[32] Although over half of the respondents believed that their lives would have been better if they had taken the alternative path at such a juncture, an encouraging 45% believed that there was no point dwelling on what could have been. One optimistic way to interpret this may be that *sliding doors moments* really are all around us, even if there is little value in spending too much time on how things might have panned out in another life.

Take the red pill

To choose to become more aware about a situation, learning the potentially unpleasant truth rather than remaining blissfully ignorant.

The Matrix, released to huge acclaim in 1999, was groundbreaking for a number of reasons, but its influence on modern philosophy is perhaps one of its lesser acknowledged contributions. The film tells the story of a young computer hacker who discovers that the world he inhabits is not real; instead it is a computer simulation, created by a set of machines who have enslaved humanity to use as a power source. *The Matrix* of the title refers to the computer-generated world created to keep humans in blissful ignorance whilst they remain hooked up to technology designed to harvest the bioelectricity they produce. In the real world, a small group of freedom fighters seek out new recruits to the cause, entering the Matrix to free humans who want to join the fight against the machines. The film's hero is Neo (played by Keanu Reeves), who turns out to be "the One" destined to free humanity from this imprisonment. Desperate to learn the truth, Neo (still in the Matrix, and still unaware that the world he inhabits is an illusion) seeks out and finds the mysterious Morpheus (Laurence Fishburne), who offers him a choice: swallow a blue pill and continue his unaware but safe former life, or take a red pill and learn the truth about what the Matrix really is. Fortunately for the plot, Neo *takes the red pill* and is awoken, allowing him to learn the horrifying truth and begin the epic fightback against the machines.

The idea of choosing between coloured potions as a way of electing to continue a journey or wake up and go back home is evident in other works, most notably *Alice's Adventures in Wonderland*, whose influence on the Matrix has been widely discussed. Despite this, the phrase *take the red pill* has since gained prominence as a marker of awakening, in the sense of choosing to learn the often unpleasant or undesirable truth about a situation, rather than opting to willingly ignore it. Modern use encompasses everything from conspiracy theories to climate change to the realities of day to day living, and could in many ways be considered as synonymous with the concept of being (or becoming) "woke" (meaning "aware of issues regarding social justice or inequality"), which gained widespread usage following the emergence of the Black Lives Matter campaign in 2013 and 2014.

An unexpected alternative use of the phrase emerged as part of the controversial men's rights movement, where *taking the red pill* has come to be used by some to refer to the realisation that, contrary to what many may claim, the modern world inherently discriminates against males in a variety of ways. A 2013 article exploring the topic cited one (unnamed) men's rights activist as saying: "Until you know *the red pill* you exist in the world of shadows and lies. You are a slave to the matriarchy."[33] Documentary film *The Red Pill* (2016) features filmmaker Cassie Jaye shadowing the leaders of the men's rights movement in the USA over the course of a year as they fight their modern crusade. The film discusses a range of issues relating to both the place of men in the modern world and the role of feminism, with (predictably) tensions high on both sides. For those who remain understandably unconvinced, Rebecca Reid's article on the *Red Pill* argument from 2015 helps to remind us that to most people it remains just a theory, and a pretty flimsy one at that.[34]

Up to 11 / turned up to 11
Something increased beyond its normal limits.

The concept of something going *up to 11* will be familiar to anyone who has seen the cult 1984 rockumentary *This is Spinal Tap*. The film is a parody of the excesses of rock bands of the time, and follows the fictional British heavy metal band Spinal Tap on a concert tour of the USA, interweaving on-the-road footage and excerpts from live performances with interviews with band members. In one such exchange, lead guitarist Nigel Tufnel (played by Christopher Guest) proudly shows off his equipment and demonstrates how the head of his amplifier is "very special" as the numbers on the various dials "all *go to 11*" rather than the traditional ten. When the interviewer asks if that makes the amp louder, Tufnel replies, "Well, it's one louder, isn't it" and goes on to explain that when they need "that extra push over the cliff" turning *up to 11* gives them the option to do so. The ridiculousness of the idea is highlighted when the interviewer goes on to ask why they wouldn't just make ten a little louder, if this was what the band required. Tufnel pauses to consider the question before answering, nonplussed, "These *go to 11*."

The original (parodic) use was to highlight that even if things are labelled or viewed in different ways, they are still essentially the same (full volume is full volume, regardless of the scale that is applied). This potentially deep philosophical insight seems to have become lost as usage of the phrase has developed, and now *turned up to 11* has come to be used almost exclusively at face value: to refer to something being increased beyond its normal limits, more or less in the spirit of how Tufnel meant it. Even those entirely unacquainted with the movie will presumably have little difficulty interpreting it in context, given how commonly we use a ten-point scale for judging the worth of just about anything (although the use of 11 as a maximum value does pre-date *This is Spinal Tap* by some time, with the Chesapeake and Ohio Railway company releasing a steam locomotive with a maximum throttle setting of 11 in 1947). As if to prove the point, the Internet Movie Database (IMDb) allows users to rate all movies on a scale from 1 to 10 stars, with no prizes for guessing which is the only film to be listed with a rating out of 11.

Almost all modern uses seem to bear out the "beyond

normal limits" meaning. Common examples include sporting performances, live music shows, TV and film, in each case being used to describe something that has greatly exceeded usual expectations or standards in some way. Other examples of things being turned *up to 11* present a much wider range of contexts, including the rise of neo-Nazi movements in the USA, an increase in nationalist feeling on the other side of the Atlantic following the Brexit vote, climate change, and even the dangers of obsessive dedication to healthy eating in a relatively new eating disorder, "Orthorexia", which is explained as "clean eating dialled *up to eleven*".[35]

As testament to the popularity of both the original film and the phrase itself, one final piece of trivia is worth noting. In 2011, Yahoo News flagged up the movement by Spinal Tap fans to ensure that 11th November (or 11/11/11) was celebrated as "Nigel Tufnel Day". Whilst not entirely sure what one was supposed to do to mark the occasion, one Yahoo News writer liked to imagine that, "it's a day to do whatever you normally do – only do it a little better. Take a look at your regular chores, your job, your schoolwork, and crank your enthusiasm *up to eleven*. Extreme elevenness, that's the goal. Oh, and play a lot of loud music too."[36] Sounds like the kind of thing Tufnel would have approved of, even if we will have to wait until the early 22nd century for another one to come around.

The usual suspects

The set of people or things that are usually associated with an event.

Perhaps more widely recognised as the title of a film in its own right, *the usual suspects* is originally a quotation from the substantially older *Casablanca*, released in 1942. *Casablanca* centres around American Rick Blaine (Humphrey Bogart), who owns a nightclub in French-controlled Casablanca during World War II. When his ex-lover and her freedom-fighting husband show up, Blaine must contend with both Major Strasser, the

German officer intent on catching them, and the corrupt local police chief, Renault. The film ends with Blaine shooting Strasser to allow the fugitives to escape Casablanca by plane, in full view of Renault. Rather than arrest Blaine, Renault instead orders his men to "round up *the usual suspects*", before suggesting that both men leave to join the Free French Forces in Brazzaville (another French colony in Africa). As quotations go, *the usual suspects* is up against some pretty stiff competition given the other memorable lines from *Casablanca* that dominate lists of favourite quotations. The AFI list alone has six separate entries (the most of any film), headed by "Here's looking at you, kid" and also featuring one of the most misquoted lines in cinema: "Play it, Sam. Play 'As Time Goes By'" (often misrepresented as "Play it again, Sam").[37] *Casablanca* itself won three Academy Awards (including Best Picture) and appears regularly on lists of the best films, including ranking number one on the AFI's "100 Years… 100 Passions" list of the greatest love stories in the history of American cinema.

Despite this popularity, The Phrase Finder suggests that aside from a small number of uses from the 1950s onward, *the usual suspects* doesn't really emerge as a common phrase until the 1990s, attributing the rise in popularity to the eponymous 1995 American thriller directed by Bryan Singer.[38] Singer, in collaboration with screenwriter Christopher McQuarrie, is reported to have taken the title from a column in satirical magazine *Spy*, based in New York and published in the USA from 1986 to 1998. *Spy* poked fun at the American media and entertainment industries, in particular lampooning Donald Trump long before anyone else took aim at him as President.[39] Amongst other regular features, "*The Usual Suspects*" was a column that rounded up celebrity goings on in a less than flattering way. Google Books digitised the *Spy* magazine archive in 2011, so readers can now see for themselves what satire looked like before the Internet made it easy to poke fun of any and everything.

The usual suspects appears in several online dictionaries, and is now often defined as the set of people or things normally associated with a particular activity. Some sources suggest that, at least when applied to criminal behaviour, this refers to scapegoats who might routinely be blamed for or sought in response to something happening, which is in keeping with the original usage in *Casablanca*. Other, broader uses apply the term to the normal things you might associate with a situation, for example in a 2004 medical paper entitled, "Coronary heart disease (CHD) in lupus: round up *the usual suspects*?", and many other articles riffing on the idea that *the usual suspects* are really only part of the problem. This perhaps gives us a further extension of the phrase: an indication that in any given situation, the well-known, widely understood facts may only tell a fraction of the story.

You're gonna need a bigger boat

An indication that a situation has been underestimated, or that the task in hand is going to require a bigger tool or different approach.

Released in 1975, *Jaws* is often considered to be one of the first summer blockbusters. The piece of dialogue that most people will forever associate with the movie (coming in at number 35 on the AFI list of memorable quotes, and number 3 on the *Hollywood Reporter* list) is uttered by the film's protagonist, police chief Martin Brody, played by Roy Scheider, who sets out to hunt down a killer shark that is terrorising the residents of fictional New England resort town Amity Island. Midway through the film, whilst Brody is throwing bait into the water to lure the shark, it appears without warning behind him, giving the audience their first glimpse of the monster. Stunned at the size of what they are hunting, Brody staggers backward and is silent for a few seconds before telling the ship's captain, Quint, *"You're gonna need a bigger boat."*

As with so many iconic movie moments, the origin of the line is apparently something of a happy accident, arising out of an in-joke that developed on set during shooting. In 2016 the *Hollywood Reporter* interviewed screenwriter Carl Gottlieb, who joined the production at the request of director Steven Spielberg to help redraft the script, which had been written by the author of the original novel, Peter Benchley.[40] Gottlieb claimed that the movie's producers, Richard Zanuck and David Brown, were "very stingy", and were reluctant to spend any money unless absolutely necessary. One particular example of this was the barge used to carry the lighting and camera equipment, which was itself supported by a much smaller boat that was simply not up to the task. The producers were repeatedly told by members of the crew, "*you're gonna need a bigger boat*", and Gottlieb goes on to recall that this "became a catchphrase for anytime anything went wrong" on set. He adds that Scheider ad-libbed the line at various points during the shooting of the movie, ultimately resulting in the perfect combination of visual astonishment and verbal understatement.

Much like composer John Williams' minimalist and terrifying theme music, *gonna need a bigger boat* has been repurposed many times, often applied to any situation where an alternative approach is required (and when such a conclusion seems all too obvious). TV Tropes lists *you're gonna need a bigger boat* as a prime example of what it calls "Dramatic Deadpan", where "a major announcement is made more dramatic by being said in a matter of fact tone".[41] Certainly part of the impact of *gonna need a bigger boat* comes from its understated delivery, and plenty of examples exist of the line being used verbatim, and in slightly more creative ways. One such use cropped up in an advert released by wood stain and paint manufacturer Ronseal in 2015 (see *Does what it says on the tin*, Chapter 2), when the necessity of coming up with a new, awkwardly long slogan for their products led to the conclusion, "*We're gonna need a bigger tin*".

Concerning the "spygate" scandal in 2018, when Donald Trump claimed that the Obama administration had been responsible for placing a Democrat spy in his 2016 Presidential election campaign team, one writer suggested that if Trump carried on in the same way then a new term would be required to describe the shenanigans associated with his presidency, concluding: "One thing is for sure, *we're going to need a bigger gate.*"[42] One UK supermarket even got in on the act with an advertisement in summer 2019, telling customers that to take home all their amazing special offers, "*You're going to need a bigger boot.*" Such uses perhaps show us that *gonna need a bigger X* now exists as a template in itself, where X can be filled as required for humorous effect. If that has happened, then we can be pretty sure that a phrase is firmly embedded in the language (see *X is my middle name*, Chapter 7, for more on this).

As the credits roll, we see a range of phrases that have undoubtedly made the leap from the big screen to the language at large. We could include plenty of other famous lines that will, for many, forever be associated with particular scenes or characters: the confrontational response *Did I stutter?* (indicating that a person does not intend to repeat her or himself), popularised by Judd Nelson in 1985 movie *The Breakfast Club*, or the taunt *how do you like them/those apples?*, apparently first used in World War I but introduced to a new audience when it was used by Matt Damon in 1997's *Good Will Hunting*. Another example of movie vocabulary that has influenced the way we communicate might be the "not joke", made famous by Mike Myers in *Wayne's World* (and although *Wayne's World* and the gag began as a skit on TV's *Saturday Night Live*, the movie undoubtedly reached a much bigger audience). Myers was also responsible for a host of memorable catchphrases from his Austin Powers movies (see *X is my middle name*, Chapter 7), in the process introducing American audiences to a host of British slang (although whether "shagadelic" was ever really a part of British English is open to question).[43]

4

Breaking the Internet: Idioms from the Online World

Richard Dawkins, renowned evolutionary biologist and writer, first coined the term "meme" in his book *The Selfish Gene* in 1976.[1] In Chapter 11 entitled "Memes: The New Replicators", he suggested that "cultural transmission is analogous to genetic transmission", hence memes (an abbreviation of the Greek mimeme, meaning "something imitated") are to culture what genes are to other aspects of human evolution. He defined memes as cultural ideas or phenomena that spread from individual to individual, giving examples such as "tunes, ideas, catchphrases, clothes, fashions, ways of making pots or of building arches".

Four decades later the idea of the meme is alive and well, specifically in the form of the Internet meme. The interminable rise of social media in the 21st century has meant that the ability to share almost anything is now literally at people's fingertips, although the term pre-dates much of the social media explosion and was first used in relation to the Internet in 1994 by Mike Godwin (of *Godwin's Law* fame, this chapter). Original Internet memes – images, short clips or simple animations – were spread via email or message boards, but the launch of YouTube (2005), followed by the emergence of Facebook (launched in 2004 and opened to the public in 2006) and Twitter (2006) opened up a world of possibilities and most Internet users have never looked back. Richard Dawkins re-entered the debate in 2013, suggesting that for Internet memes to be true to his original formulation, they would need to be somehow changed and mutated during the process of transmission. For many, this is exactly the point: taking an original idea and putting a unique stamp on it, often as a way of expressing emotion or reacting to a major event. The protracted saga of Brexit, for example, was fertile ground, and a BBC News article in 2019 asked whether memes were a necessary response to turbulent political times, as a way of releasing the tension that might otherwise build up.[2] Priceonomics, a company that specialises in creating viral online content, agreed, and their analysis showed huge increases in the number of memes with political or ideological features as of 2016, when the Trump election campaign went into overdrive in the USA.[3]

In some ways, memes are the Internet version of idioms. They emerge, often in response to a particular event or from a particular subculture, and slowly but surely make their way around the world (virtually, at least). Predictably, many die a death pretty soon afterward, but some survive to make the leap from the language of the Internet to the language in general. Not all of the entries in this chapter constitute memes, but all are expressions or phrases that have either begun life online, emerging from Internet discussions or notable events, or have been popularised and proliferated through digital transmission.

Break the Internet

To cause massive reaction and interest online.

Break the Internet has undergone something of a transformation during its life to date. Initially the term was used at face value: Merriam-Webster online reported that the first usage it could find was from 1996, with a reassurance from a Training and Development article on the subject of using web browsers that, "You can't *break the internet*," meaning, literally, that it was not possible to cause any lasting damage simply by using a browser badly.[4] Other early uses focused on the ability to crash a web server by directing huge amounts of traffic to it, or discussions of the balance that needed to be struck between keeping the Internet freely accessible to all, and "breaking it", either by adding in protections that would inevitably slow it down to a crawl, or by fundamentally changing the nature of how it operated. British TV sitcom *The IT Crowd* (see *Have you tried turning it off and on again?*, Chapter 2) parodied the idea that anyone could actually *break the Internet* on two occasions. In one episode, IT experts Roy and Moss play a trick on their computer-illiterate boss, Jen, by presenting her with "the Internet" – a small black box with a blinking red light on it – to display to a meeting of company shareholders. When a scuffle breaks out and the box is knocked to the floor, smashing it beyond repair, mass panic follows as everyone is convinced that this will be the end of civilisation as they know it. On a different occasion, the pair convince Jen to warn a group of board members, "if you type 'Google' into Google, you can *break the Internet*." Despite scepticism, Jen assures the executives that this is a real danger, asking that "no one try it, even for a joke". Thankfully this myth was safely debunked in an article from 2011, which confirmed that typing "Google" into Google did very little other than return search results for the term itself.[5]

In modern usage the term has acquired both a more positive and a more figurative spin: something that *breaks the Internet* these days is an occurrence that dominates the online conversation, provoking huge interest or reaction and swamping social media. The Merriam-Webster article cited above was part of its "Words We're Watching" series, on words that seemed to be growing in usage, even if they hadn't yet become widespread enough for full entry into the dictionary. It cites an early usage from a 2001 issue of *Time Out* magazine, when the Conran Shop launched a new website and eager shoppers were warned, "don't all rush on at once as you might *break the internet*." Certainly this seems to be the first extension of the phrase to reflect the idea that a sudden rush of interest might overload servers and bring a website to a grinding halt.

The article also reports on the inaugural awarding (in 2016) of the "*Break the Internet*" award at the Webbys, an annual celebration of the "best of the Internet" by the International Academy of Digital Arts and Sciences. The award was for, "A person with an undeniable talent and natural ability to use the Internet to create buzz, engage with fans and communities, and get the world to pay attention." The Webby committee chose to honour Kim Kardashian-West with the first iteration of such an honour, citing "her unparalleled success online" in *breaking the Internet* and putting it back together in her likeness".[6] Certainly one of the best-known examples of *breaking the Internet* had featured Kardashian-West two years previously, when *Paper* magazine featured her on the cover of its winter 2014 issue. The magazine explicitly stated that it had given itself "one assignment: To *break the Internet*" and it certainly gave this a good try. The cover image (along with the headline "*Break the Internet*") featured Kardashian-West showing off her very nude buttocks, and quickly gained notoriety online: the day after the story was published the magazine's website received 6.6 million visits, with a further 15.9 million the following day. *Time* magazine featured the publication as the first item in its "Top 10 Things That *Broke the Internet*" in 2014, claiming that "Kim did not literally *break the Internet*, but she came very close".[7]

Collateral knowledge / collateral information

Information learned as a by-product of researching or reading up on something else.

Collateral knowledge or *collateral information* already has a well-established meaning (or set of meanings) in the world of finance. Fairly transparently, *collateral knowledge* is information gathered on the subject of financial collateral, with multiple works dedicated to this specialised topic. An alternative meaning exists in both legal and medical terms, relating to information gathered as a by-product of another course of investigation. In psychiatry or social work, *collateral information* may be the information gathered about a person by talking to their family, friends and other contacts.

Elsewhere, *collateral knowledge* has acquired a different nuance. Urban Dictionary provides an entry for this, clarifying that *collateral knowledge* is information learned accidentally whilst attempting to research or learn about something else entirely. In particular, the phrase seems most applicable in the context of Wikipedia, where readers can easily "chain" from one article to another, thereby quickly and easily learning about an array of subjects that may be far removed from the originally intended topic. Various names for this phenomenon have been applied, such as the idea of going down a "wiki rabbit hole" or "wiki black hole", and the pastime has even developed into a (semi) competitive sport, in the form of "wikiracing" or "the Wiki Game".[8] Here, competitors must aim to traverse Wikipedia by making use of links to reach a specified finish page in either the shortest amount of time or the fewest clicks. An alternative pastime exists in the form of Six Degrees of Wikipedia, which aims to find the shortest chains between two seemingly unconnected Wikipedia articles.[9] The idea is a variation on the theme of "six degrees of separation", which suggests that all people are linked by no more than six social connections (or if you prefer, the evolution of the idea into "Six Degrees of Kevin Bacon" or simply "Bacon's Law", suggesting that any Hollywood star can be linked to actor Kevin Bacon via a limited number of shared film roles). Unofficial "rules" of the game include that links must not be "uninteresting", and that users must not tamper with articles solely for the purpose of changing the degrees of separations between two pages.

Such potential for underhand behaviour leads to the related concept of *collateral misinformation*. Urban Dictionary and several other sources provide an explanation that this is the result of someone altering a Wikipedia article in order to win an argument, in the process laying open the possibility that other readers may come across and take as accurate the error before it can be corrected.[10] More broadly, *collateral misinformation* can be seen as any misleading "fact" that is repeated to the point where it becomes accepted as true. Comedian Alex Horne (see *Mental safari*, Chapter 7) cites an example of just this in his 2010 book *Wordwatching*, when a rumour that he had started regarding his own early forays into comedy (he claimed that he became a comedian after he won a competition to create the best Christmas cracker joke) was repeated as fact on ITV. Of course, in a world where fake news is now a well-known and widespread part of modern life, *collateral misinformation* may be far more common than we realise. "Fake news" itself was crowned word of the year by Collins Dictionary and the American Dialect Society in 2017 (and by the Macquarie Dictionary in Australia in 2016), and itself might be considered an idiom given that it effectively has two meanings: the first, a literal description of deliberate fabrication, and the second, a dismissive accusation made by anyone to describe news that they don't particularly like. Coming hot on the heels of "post-truth" being named Oxford English Dictionary word of the year in 2016, it seems the potential for *collateral misinformation* is not about to go away any time soon.

First world problems

Problems or annoyances that are sarcastically acknowledged to be comparatively minor compared to issues elsewhere in the world.

Perhaps the clearest example of a Twitter hashtag becoming an idiom, *first world problems* now appears in several dictionaries, including, as of 2012, the Oxford English Dictionary, where it is defined as "a relatively trivial or minor problem", in contrast to the serious issues faced by those living in other parts of the world.[11] The term makes what looks to be its first appearance in an article from 1979 entitled "Housing: Third World Solutions to *First World Problems*".[12] The piece had a very different idea in mind, however, than the way the phrase has come to be used as a way of either shaming those who complain about perceived "problems", or as a way for someone to ironically mock their own privilege. The kinds of things that often appear on lists of *first world problems* include slow Internet access (the number one concern amongst New Zealanders in a poll conducted in 2012),[13] forgetting to check your pockets for paper before washing your clothes (listed as number one in 21 Truly Devastating *First World Problems* in a 2014 BuzzFeed list)[14] and, somewhat pathetically, having a runny nose (apparently the number one complaint of most respondents in a 2015 survey of Britons).

Several sources report that the phrase itself first appeared in the lyrics of the song *Omissions of the Omen* by Canadian musicians the Matthew Good Band, released in 1995. Possibly unconnected, an article from 1999 in the *South China Morning Post* cited concerns of residents at Discovery Bay (an upmarket development in Hong Kong) about the "distastefully dressed" security guards, which the writer describes as *"First World Problems."*[15] The term first appeared on Urban Dictionary in 2005, and grew in popularity from there, primarily thanks to its use on Twitter, but also thanks to various other platforms such as Tumblr, Reddit and BuzzFeed, which utilised various image-based jokes as a way of spreading the meme. Know Your Meme also lists several derivatives – including "Third World Success" as "the antithesis of *first world problems*" – and also cites web statistics that suggest a peak usage of the hashtag on Twitter in July 2011.[16] An alternative name – "White Whine" – was also coined, possibly by American comedian Streeter Seidell, who launched a Twitter account of the same name in 2009, followed by a website (now defunct) and book: *White Whine: A Study of First-World Problems* (published in 2013), each presenting a very tongue-in cheek collection of "the everyday difficulties that plague our lives".

US-based charity Water is Life tapped into the phenomenon in a 2012 campaign featuring poverty-stricken residents of Haiti reading out tweets with the *first world problems* hashtag, before demonstrating their own challenges in response. Although some were quick to point out that the ironic nature of the complaints seemed to have been ignored, the campaign was seen by others as a valuable opportunity.[17] In 2014 Computer Aid International launched its own campaign – *First World Pennies* – to encourage people to share money, rather than complaints. The *Mirror* online, reporting on the campaign, suggested that at the time 5,000 tweets per day used the hashtag *first world problems*.[18] But not everyone is agreed on the morality of *first world problems*. Some see it as condescending, reinforcing fundamental divisions between Western and supposedly "undeveloped" nations. Others highlight how cathartic it can be to "check your privilege" – itself a meme that grew in popularity from its first usage in around 2006 – and understand how (comparatively) lucky we are, just as long as we then go on to do some good as a result. As Sara Cox, writing in 2015, put it, "you can have a grumble, just make sure you put your money where your moan is."[19]

Godwin's Law

The maxim that the longer an argument goes on, the more likely it is that one of the people involved will compare the opposing side to the Nazis.

Godwin's Law, also known as *Godwin's Law of Nazi Analogies* or "The Sexton-Godwin Law", was first formulated by attorney and writer Mike Godwin in 1990, in relation to online conversations using Usenet newsgroups. Usenet newsgroups were early discussion platforms, similar in principle to later Internet forums, and *Godwin's Law* has subsequently become applicable to any discussion, online or offline, where arguments become more heated over time. The law states: "As an online discussion grows longer, the probability of a comparison involving Nazis or Hitler approaches one". Or, put another way, the longer a discussion goes on, the more likely it is that someone will resort to a comparison with fascism as a way of trying to win the argument. Godwin himself has stated that the initial coinage was an exercise in "mimetic engineering", in response to the fact that he perceived Nazi analogies popping up in discussions of all kinds of topics online, which "trivialised the horror of the Holocaust and the social pathology of the Nazis".[20] To Godwin's delight, his counter-meme spread, mutated and spawned a range of similar maxims. A development of the idea states that once *Godwin's Law* has been invoked, the discussion itself no longer serves any useful purpose, as the level of debate has fallen too low for it to make any further meaningful contribution.

Godwin was not the first to identify the use of Hitler comparisons as a common rhetorical tool. Back in the 1950s political philosopher Leo Strauss coined the term "reduction ad Hitlerum" ("reduction to Hitler") as a description of the nonsensical tactic of discrediting someone's argument by comparing it to the behaviour of Hitler and the Nazis. Especially in the USA, "reduction ad Stalinum" or "red-baiting" has also been a method of attacking another's argument by comparing it specifically to Communist ideals, and was even used in the UK in the 21st century, by then Mayor of London Boris Johnson to describe the proposed introduction of a higher rate of tax for top earners.[21] Godwin himself has commented on the law over the years, stating that his explicit intention was to encourage people who used the Nazi comparison freely and frivolously to put a little more thought into their choice of words. On the 18th anniversary of the emergence of *Godwin's Law*, its creator wrote that, "we have a moral obligation to prevent such events from ever happening again. Key to that obligation is remembering, which is what *Godwin's Law* is all about."[22]

Godwin's Law, although one of the earliest, is far from the only maxim that exists regarding Internet behaviour. Tom Chivers rounded up ten of the most important rules in 2009 (so there may well be others to abide by now), starting with *Godwin's Law*, and including such others as "Danth's Law" ("If you have to insist that you've won an Internet argument, you've probably lost badly") and "The Law of Exclamation" ("The more exclamation points used in an email (or other posting), the more likely it is a complete lie. This is also true for excessive capital letters.").[23] None have quite taken on a life of their own like *Godwin's Law*, however, which was added to the Oxford English Dictionary in 2012, cementing its place in the lexicon.

Keyboard warrior

Someone who engages in confrontational, aggressive and often abusive behaviour online.

The contribution of the Internet and social media to how we communicate has been transformative, but not always in a good way. The availability of information means that (in theory) people can be more connected than ever before, but this also means that almost anyone can have a platform to either espouse their own views, or comment on those of other people. From here the term *keyboard warrior* emerged, referring to anyone happy to engage in combative and often downright offensive exchanges online. An implication is that in most cases the same people would never behave in the same way in real life, and so are using the veil of anonymity offered by the computer screen as a way to express themselves with relative impunity.

Urban Dictionary cites a definition added in 2006 (an earlier one exists from February 2005), clarifying that *keyboard warriors* "are generally identified by unnecessary rage in their written communications, and are regarded as 'losers' by other virtual identities on the internet."[24] Beyond these, a 2008 interview with heavy metal singer Mandy Lion provides one of the earliest written uses of the term. In response to a question about how he felt about his polarising effect on music fans, Lion said, "For every bad reaction I get thousands of good reactions so I never sweat the couple of web sites where 'keyboard warriors' leave their ever so important opinions."[25]

Other uses of the phrase reflect slightly different nuances, such as British hacker Lauri Love who was described as a *keyboard warrior* in the title of an article reporting on his fight against extradition to the USA for "criminal hacking", including his alleged role in a cyber-attack by Anonymous on USA government websites.[26] (Love subsequently won an appeal against extradition in 2018.) The description was also applied during the protracted protests in Hong Kong in 2019, when *keyboard warriors* were accused of "besieging Wikipedia".[27] Users apparently used the platform to rewrite pages on Hong Kong's government and police force, "swapped facts for insults", and generally sought to "upset the balance of articles", including at one point changing the motto quoted on the Hong Kong police page from "We Serve with Pride and Care" to "We Serve with Terror and Violence".

The idea of the *keyboard warrior* has also been applied in the world of online activism, where the ease with which people can engage with causes and debates has, some argue, changed the face of public participation in the 21st century. An analysis of the political-activism organisation 38 Degrees suggested that its success in "mobilising public participation" came in energising members through a genuine sense that they could make a contribution, debunking the "myth of the *keyboard warrior*".[28] Others argue just as stridently that "clicktivism" or "slacktivism" allows people to feel good about supporting political causes online without actually having to go to too much effort to do so. Whichever way we look at it, *keyboard warriors* show no signs of laying down their weapons any time soon.

Milkshake duck

Something that enjoys very rapid success or popularity, but which then experiences an equally rapid backlash when an initially unknown flaw is discovered.

Milkshake duck first emerged as an Internet meme in June 2016, after Australian cartoonist Ben Ward (better known on Twitter as @pixelatedboat) tweeted: "The whole internet loves *Milkshake Duck*, a lovely duck that drinks milkshakes! *5 seconds later* We regret to inform you that the duck is racist". Ward's intention was to reflect a growing trend whereby the Internet can bring rapid attention and popularity, but can just as quickly lead to a very speedy backlash when past indiscretions or unsavoury opinions are uncovered. Urban Dictionary's entry, added in June 2017, clarifies that a *milkshake duck* is someone who enjoys sudden fame that is generally very positive, but that "a deeply flawed character with terrible opinions and/or a shady past, often involving corrosive social/political ideologies" quickly lead to a turning of the Internet tide.[29] To cap off its meteoric rise, *milkshake duck* was even declared word of the year for 2017 by The Macquarie Dictionary in Australia.

Several well-known examples are often cited as part of this digital-age cautionary tale.[30] Keaton Jones, a young man from Tennessee, made a video about being bullied that garnered immediate and widespread support, only for allegations about his family's questionable views on race to emerge and quickly muddy the waters of public opinion. Ken Bone, an attendee who asked a question about energy policy at one of the presidential debates in 2016, was taken into the hearts of Americans everywhere, until Internet users uncovered a series of unsavoury posts that Bone had made on a variety of subjects in the past, quickly changing public perception. Policeman Michael Hamill (aka Florida Hot Cop) uploaded a photo of himself and two colleagues to Facebook that was widely swooned over, only for previous comments to come out following which Hamill decided to remove himself from his position. Finally, Candace Payne, better known across the Internet as "Chewbacca Mask Lady", uploaded a video of herself laughing uncontrollably at a mask of *Star Wars* character Chewbacca. The Internet found her enjoyment so amusing that numerous TV appearances and multiple endorsements soon followed. However, despite no past actions coming out of the woodwork to trip her up, people soon became unimpressed by the extent to which Payne seemed to be exploiting her new-found fame. By the time she released a new video – her singing Michael Jackson's *Heal the World* in December 2016 – the backlash was complete, and the Internet decided that it had heard quite enough of "Chewbacca Mom", as she became known.

As proof that nothing stands still on the Internet, toward the end of 2018 an evolution emerged in the form of a *reverse milkshake duck*. A Florida-based Twitter user posted a picture of her son along with the hashtag #HimToo, which emerged as a pushback against the widespread #MeToo movement against sexual harassment and abuse of women. The implication of the post was that her son was scared to go on dates anymore because of the fear of false accusations, and immediately afterward the son in question, Pieter Hanson, felt compelled to open his own Twitter account in order to point out that the picture his mother was painting was sadly misguided, and to state his absolute opposition to the #HimToo campaign. He was nice about it, and rather than tearing his mother down simply wrote, "Sometimes the people we love do things that hurt us without realizing it" (although he reportedly did say of the original Tweet, "at the end of the day we all have crazy parents"). In an article reporting the story, *Guardian* writer Luke O'Neill suggested that this may be "one of the first instances of the reversal [of *Milkshake duck*]", where initial outrage is replaced by a wave of positive feelings toward the subject.[31]

For those wanting to see the rollercoaster journey of *milkshake duck* for themselves, original creator Ben Ward did post a follow-up cartoon, "The Rise and Fall of *Milkshake Duck*" in December 2017. Available on comics publication website The Nib, the story shows our hero's descent into milkshake-fuelled ignominy, culminating in the realisation that as a meme, all he would be remembered as was "the Duck That Drank Milkshakes And Was Also Racist". Did he deserve his fate, he muses? "How the hell would [he] know: [he's] just a duck that likes milkshakes."[32]

Netflix and chill

A euphemism for sexual activity, under the guise of inviting someone over to watch on-demand TV.

Netflix and chill started life as a fairly innocent and entirely transparent description of an evening's activities. Although now one of the most widely used streaming services offering easy access to TV and movie content via the Internet, Netflix began as a DVD-by-mail order rental company in the late-1990s. By 2007, on the back of the success enjoyed by YouTube, Netflix launched its streaming service and the video-on-demand model quickly became the new way forward. *Netflix and chill* first emerged two years later, when one Twitter user posted in January 2009 that she was going to "log onto *Netflix and chill* for the rest of the night". Over the next few years, the phrase proliferated on social media, and as Netflix became its own verb (just like Google before it), *Netflix and chill* became a common way to describe your plans for the evening.

By 2014, euphemism and innuendo began to creep in, and the phrase acquired its new meaning. *Netflix and chill* became a byword for "romantic" activity, or "a 21st-century version of 'Do you want to come up for some coffee?'"[33] Various sources suggest that the phrase began life amongst the African-American Twitter community, or "Black Twitter", with rapid, more widespread adoption on social media platforms, memes, a huge surge in Internet searches, and an Urban Dictionary entry in 2015 all cementing the new, alternative meaning. Netflix acknowledged the joke itself in July 2015, and later that year launched a prototype electronic device called "The Switch" (quickly dubbed the *Netflix and chill* button) – a controller that could be rigged up to automatically dim your lights, set your phone to "Do Not Disturb" and start queuing up your favourite shows ready for streaming. One entrepreneur cashed in on the phenomenon by launching a brand of *Netflix and chill* condoms, making it rather harder to argue that the phrase was an innocent invitation. Around the same time, articles began to emerge highlighting how transparent the "nudge-nudge context of *Netflix and chill*" had become (see *Nudge nudge, wink wink*, Chapter 2), in the process ruining things for those who genuinely just wanted to enjoy a night of good TV.[34]

As well as Urban Dictionary, both Macmillan Dictionary online and Dictionary.com now list the euphemistic meaning. Dictionary.com even provides an alternative, with one Twitter user from 2017 professing, "I'm too old for *Netflix and chill*. Now I want Amazon Prime and commitment."[35] Although not the first person to adapt things in this way, this was certainly more subtle than some of the modifications proposed elsewhere (Amazon Prime and sexy time, anyone?). Whatever the euphemism, it is generally agreed that once parents and the wider world begin to cotton on, the joke has almost certainly run its course.

OK, boomer

A phrase used to dismiss or mock someone of the baby-boomer generation for expressing ideas seen as out-of-touch or condescending.

OK, boomer shot to prominence in 2019 as a rallying cry for the younger generations who were tired of being lectured by so-called "baby boomers" (generally people who grew up in the decades following World War II). The phrase was used in response to a post on video sharing site TikTok, where an unidentified older white male ranted about what he called "Peter Pan syndrome" amongst millennials and members of Generation Z. The response was instant, as users waded in to comment using the tag *OK, boomer* to dismiss what were seen as out-of-date ideals and tired, predictable criticisms. A raft of articles on the topic helped to catapult it into the public eye, and by the end of 2019 *OK, boomer* was a firm fixture on a host of web platforms.

Plenty of interest in the phrase helps us to see how it first came about, and how it subsequently spread like the proverbial wildfire. Know Your Meme reports that the exact origins are unknown, but that uses were seen as early as 2015 (on imageboard forum 4chan), 2017 (on news aggregation site Reddit), and then by 2018 on Twitter. One analysis reports that *OK, boomer* first appeared on Reddit as early as 2009, but that an upsurge in usage did not begin until ten years later in 2019.[36] A spike in September of that year followed (when a group of teenagers launched a petition on Reddit to change the word "old" to the word "boomer"), then once *The New York Times* published an article on the topic, claiming that "*OK Boomer* marks the end of friendly generational relationships", use (on Reddit at least) skyrocketed. By 4th November, New Zealand member of parliament Chlöe Swarbrick (who was 25 years old at the time) hit the headlines when she used *OK, boomer* as a retort to being heckled during a speech about climate change. In response to the general rise of the phrase, boomers hit back, with some claiming that it was ageist, and one conservative American radio host, Bob Lonsberry, even going as far as to describe it as "the n-word of ageism".[37] When a predictable backlash ensued, he hastily deleted the Tweet expressing this opinion.

Strong opinions rage on both sides, and many commentators saw the phrase as far more than a throwaway putdown or simple dismissal. One article described "the most polarizing meme of the year" as showing that the younger generation were tired of being lectured and condescended to by an older generation that was perceived as having had it pretty good, and who the millennials and the Generations Z-ers blamed for many of the serious political, economic and environmental challenges that they faced. *OK, boomer* represented "an instantly relatable cry of frustration", not simply rehashing the standard conflicts between generations, but a genuine exhaustion at the (perceived) refusal of many "boomers" to understand the problems facing the generations to come.[38] As Chlöe Swarbrick, writing in the days following her unexpected rise to (temporary) Internet stardom, explained, the "off-the-cuff" comment was "symbolic of the collective exhaustion of multiple generations set to inherit ever-amplifying problems in an ever-diminishing window of time." The point, she went on, was that in order to address the biggest challenges, democracy must "look like all of us. Memes and all."[39]

Of all the chapters in this book, it seems a fair bet that this is the one that will separate readers into the "heards" and "heard nots" more than any other. Internet crazes and memes seem to erupt into life and take hold with little warning and keeping up with them all is an impossible task. The few that make it beyond the online world – often with the help of numerous articles in more established print media to help highlight a newly-coined or popularised expression – may become familiar to those who don't live their lives entirely online, but by then the younger generation will undoubtedly have moved on (as seen with *Netflix and chill*). But as the examples show, often memes are much more than just ways to share amusing images or pass the time on a slow workday. Memes provide an outlet for political or social comment that might otherwise not exist, allowing users around the world to engage in debate, share ideas, express their frustrations and show their solidarity in easy, relatable ways. Entwined in our lives as it is, the Internet is not going to stop providing sources for new words and phrases any time soon, but where the next one comes from is anyone's guess.

5

Jumpers for Goalposts: Idioms from the World of Sport

Sport has already contributed many a turn of phrase (as well as a fair number of clichés) to English. We don't have to look hard to find long lists of idioms that refer to cricket (*hit for six, on a sticky wicket, be bowled over* or *caught out, to have a good innings*), boxing (*on the ropes, hit below the belt, throw in the towel, a puncher's chance, saved by the bell, out for the count*), horse racing (*a dark horse, on the home straight, front runner, across the board, to win hands down*) and football (*score an own goal, miss an open goal, kick something off, be on the ball*). More surprising, perhaps, is the number of idioms that come from sports that are popular primarily in the USA, but which nonetheless will be familiar to most speakers of British English. Phrases such as *hit a home run* or *touch base* are generally understood by most in the UK, as is the idea of something unconventional being from *left field*, giving someone a *ball park figure, playing hardball, throwing a curve ball* or *going to bat for someone*, all derived from baseball. Similarly, describing a resounding success as a *slam dunk* will likely not confuse too many people regardless of how much basketball you watch. In contrast, American football offers a handful of choice expressions that may be less obvious in their origin, at least to those in the UK. Merriam-Webster online summarises some of these, with one (possibly) better-known example being *to run interference*, referring to a player assisting his teammate by preventing the opposition from getting to the ball; more broadly, *running interference* can refer to helping someone by distracting attention from what she or he is doing. Perhaps less common is to describe something as a *Hail Mary*, which is a last-ditch attempt at an extremely risky play in the very dying seconds of a game or, by extension, a bold and risky "do or die" move in any situation.[1]

The phrases considered in more detail in this chapter have certainly gone beyond the boundaries of their own sports (even if only to make a short leap to another one), and in some cases have gone even further to make it into more general vocabulary.

Corridor of uncertainty
A situation where the right course of action is unclear.

One that should be familiar to most followers of cricket, the *corridor of uncertainty* is an area often targeted by bowlers where the batsman is unsure of the best course of action. A ball bowled at the stumps requires the batsman to defend, otherwise he risks being bowled. In contrast, a ball bowled wide of the stumps can be safely left alone as it poses no danger (unless the batsman chooses to hit it, in which case she or he risks being caught). Anything bowled in the *corridor of uncertainty* – a narrow channel fractionally outside of the stumps – poses a problem, as the batsman cannot be certain whether to play or leave the ball. Former England batsman and later commentator Geoffrey Boycott is often associated with the phrase, and it forms part of the repertoire of stock phrases that characterise his candid approach to broadcasting. Fans of the radio institution *Test Match Special* even invented the game of "Boycott Bingo" to allow listeners to tick off their own favourite Boycott-isms, including other classics such as (of dropped catches), "My mum could have caught that in her pinny" and (of a missed shot by a batsman), "He could have hit that with a stick of rhubarb."[2]

Despite this, others have suggested that the phrase *corridor of uncertainty* pre-dates Boycott, who claimed to have come up with it "on the spot" whilst commentating in the West Indies in 1990.[3] An article from Australian newspaper *The Age*, reporting on England's struggles against Australia in July 1989, suggested that bowler Terry Alderman "rarely strayed from the '*corridor of uncertainty'* that he coined himself several years ago". It seems likely that such a phrase emerged sometime during the 1980s and began to slowly creep into the vocabulary of cricketers everywhere, helped no doubt by the no-nonsense approach taken by Boycott once he took up the microphone.

An even earlier usage, entirely unrelated to the world of cricket and from the other side of the Atlantic, was recorded in 1986, when a NASA scientist, Dr Raymond Colladay, presented a statement on the development of hydrogen as a source of fuel to a House of Representatives Subcommittee on Transportation, Aviation and Materials. During questions following his statement, Dr Colladay spoke of the difficulty of finding the best altitude when attempting to reach speeds of up to Mach 25, mentioning the *"corridor of uncertainty...* as to what the optimum flight profile will be". Since then, it has also cropped up from time to time in other contexts: in relation to newspaper editorials who took a relatively middle-ground view in the 1997 UK general election, dubbed the *corridor of uncertainty* in an analysis of national press coverage at the time;[4] and in works on economics, physics and even the production of microprocessors, where it seems to have a meaning not too far away from "margin for error".

Uses of the term now predominantly relate to cricket (including being utilised as the name of numerous fanzines, forums, and even the title of a book about the creation of the first ever Afghanistan national cricket team), and definitions of the phrase in online dictionaries (sporting and otherwise) tend to refer to it in these terms. By extension, it has made its way into another sport, and is now also commonly understood in the context of football. In these terms, the *corridor of uncertainty* might refer to an area in-between the goalkeeper and his defenders, hence a ball played in here by an attacking side might cause uncertainty as to whose responsibility it is to deal with the danger. Some dictionaries list this as an alternative or even primary meaning, although at least the list of "the most poetic phrases from the beautiful game" provided by the BBC (featuring *corridor of uncertainty* at number one) had the decency to clarify that it was "unashamedly stolen from cricket".[5]

Deep bench / bench strength

A strong supply of reserve or secondary options.

Many sports allow the use of substitutes, who originally sat on a bench at the side of the pitch, waiting to be called on by the coach. These days, highly-paid sports stars are more likely to be seated in plush luxury chairs, but the concept of a *deep bench* or alternatively *bench strength* remains the same, referring to a strong set of reserve options. The term is often applied to top teams who have a large number of very talented players, meaning that even those players left on the substitutes bench are of very high quality. In contrast, weaker teams (or those with less money!) may have fewer options, hence those players amongst the substitutes may be, by necessity, less effective. Especially in sports where rolling substitutions are allowed (such as basketball), the strategic use of a *deep bench* is often cited as a reason for success, since no arrangement of players will be weaker than any other.

Outside of sport, the term is more generally applied to situations where having a range of talented options is a good thing. One design agency described the importance of a *deep bench* in successful business, clarifying that this did not simply mean "having enough bodies to fill a meeting or drown a conference call", but that the team should be truly talented and diverse, with enough strength in depth to handle projects of any size.[6] Other businesses have followed suit, with multiple industry articles on the importance of a *deep bench* in running a successful company. The term has also been applied in political contexts, in particular referring to the *deep bench* of possible candidates for high profile roles in US politics. Journalists were quick to apply the term to the range of Republican candidates who contested the presidential primaries in 2015 (the 17 people who put their names forward for the Republicans made this the largest field in US election history), then the same term was applied to the even larger set of Democrat options in 2019.

In a much more irreverent way, satirist Andy Borowitz used the phrase to describe the political situation in North Korea. Writing about the unexplained disappearance of leader Kim Jong-un in 2014 (when he was absent from public life for six weeks), Borowitz claimed that the North Korean government had reassured its citizens of its *deep bench* of brutal madmen", meaning that it was in no danger of relying on just one man to maintain its status as the world's leading "authoritarian horror-drome".[7] As the (fictional) statement from North Korea went on to confirm, "No other government has a roster that strong."

Flat track bully

Someone who thrives when conditions are easy but struggles to do so well when put in a more challenging situation.

Another phrase that will be familiar to cricket fans, a *flat track bully* is a batsman who flourishes when the going is easy, but who struggles as soon as the conditions become more difficult. In cricketing terms, a "flat" pitch (or track) is one where with little bounce or sideways movement, hence when the bowler sends the ball down, it is unlikely to react off the surface, and is therefore less likely to cause any unforeseen difficulties for the batsman. In theory, such a pitch should be easier to score runs on than one where the ball is behaving more unpredictably, and conditions are therefore more challenging. The idea is not unrelated to a more established idiom like *make hay while the sun shines*, with the same underlying image of making the most of a favourable set of circumstances.

The term may have first been applied to Graeme Hick, who played county cricket for Worcestershire for over 20 years

(1984-2008). Hick, like many cricketers at the time, spent his winters playing for sides elsewhere in the world, and during his time playing in New Zealand (1987-88 and 1988-89) was a huge success. John Bracewell, at the time a player for the New Zealand national side, described Hick as a *flat track bully*, reflecting his voracious appetite for runs and ability to dominate the bowling. Unfortunately, despite reproducing similar form for Worcestershire on a regular basis, Hick never reached the same heights at international level. His career was dogged by Bracewell's comment, and he bowed out of international cricket after ten years in 2001 with an average of just over 31 (considerably lower than his overall average of over 50). Far from its original intention as a compliment, *flat track bully* now carries the implication that a batsman can only perform well when circumstances are favourable, or when the opposition is less accomplished.

Unsurprisingly, given the set of countries in which cricket is most popular, *flat track bully* is a term most commonly seen in the UK and Australia, where in both locations it has migrated to other sports. As well as entire football teams and even managers, rugby stars, tennis players, Australian Rules footballers and Gaelic football teams have all been labelled as such at various times. In footballing terms, the accusation of being a *flat track bully* is sometimes levelled against players who only seem to score goals against weaker opposition. In contrast, an article following the 2017-18 football season in the UK highlighted those players who were the "worst *flat-track bullies*", whose records showed that they consistently upped their games against the supposedly stronger sides (but conversely, performed much less well against "weaker" teams).[8]

Examples of the phrase do exist further afield. With reference to an ongoing stadium development project in Sydney in 2016, Australian sports minister Stuart Ayres was described as a *flat track bully* who had a tendency to only talk to media who already agreed with him, whilst avoiding scrutiny from less enthusiastic quarters.[9] Similarly, Facebook's foray into the world of streaming sports events in 2017 hit a stumbling block when it was outbid for the rights to the Indian Premier League cricket competition, leaving one Business Technology journalist to comment that it "faces challenges in becoming a *flat track bully* in the sports arena".[10] Since both pieces do have some connection to the world of sport, it seems likely that the writers in question were employing a degree of journalistic licence, but they represent evidence of a move toward wider usage nonetheless.

Go big or go home
To act boldly and put in the maximum effort (or else give up altogether).

Some uncertainty exists as to the origin of *go big or go home* (sometimes also *go hard or go home*), but it is certainly a phrase most commonly associated with the world of sport. The idea is simple: often players reach a point where they have to do something big and bold because if they don't, they may as well give up as a more cautious strategy will inevitably lead to a loss. The phrase is often used in sports such as tennis, where a player may have the best chance by playing higher-risk, more aggressive shots, rather than adopting a more passive, defensive strategy and hoping that an opponent makes mistakes.

The Grammarist website suggests several options for where this phrase first came from.[11] One suggestion is that it was a sales slogan for a motorcycle parts manufacturer who utilised it on the packaging for their oversized exhaust pipes in the 1990s. Others have claimed that the phrase was already in common usage in the vocabulary of extreme sports such as mogul skiing (freestyle skiing down a bumpy or "moguled" course) and surfing in the 1980s. Here, those taking part in these activities would compete with each other to tackle bigger and more difficult challenges (ski runs or waves, respectively), hence any participant not willing to tackle the biggest obstacles may as well not take part. Multiple sources, however, show that the phrase was already around long before either motorcycle manufacturers or skiing daredevils began to use it. Online dictionary of American slang The Big Apple cites an earlier example from the 1960s.[12] An article in Boston-based newspaper the *Traveler* from 25th February 1964 entitled "War in Vietnam is already lost" included the line, "In the language of the race-track plunger, the choice there has always been the same: *Go big or go home*". Here, "plunger" is a slang expression for a gambler, suggesting that this is another phrase that we can attribute to the world of horse-racing. The Big Apple also features examples of *go hard or go home* dating from even earlier, appearing in a College Slang Dictionary in 1942, but confirms that both versions of the phrase only became popular in the 1980s.[13]

Go big or go home is now a common phrase in many walks of life, but there is also a healthy dose of scepticism over its value as a guiding principle. Many entrepreneurial articles argue firmly against it, encouraging businesses to concentrate on building a solid, sustainable base rather than aiming too high too quickly. Will Hayes, writing on Forbes.com, made exactly this point in 2015, when he wrote about the "Age of Unicorns" that we are living in (a Unicorn being a business start-up valued at over a billion dollars). Contrary to a *go big or go home* mentality, he argued that winning takes time, and not becoming a runaway success overnight is not a mark of failure. As he put it, "Everyone's aiming to become a unicorn on steroids, but there's nothing wrong with trying to become a really beautiful horse."[14]

The hairdryer treatment
To shout forcibly and directly at someone whilst telling them off.

Sir Alex Ferguson managed Manchester United from 1986 to 2013, and is widely regarded as one of the greatest and most successful domestic football managers in the history of the English game. Several phrases have been attributed to him (see *Squeaky bum time*, this chapter), either directly or indirectly. One such example is *the hairdryer treatment*, which derives from his habit of showing his displeasure at a poor performance by shouting at players with such ferocity that it was like having a hairdryer blasted into their faces. The phrase is reported to have been coined by Mark Hughes (a former United player), and has more often been applied by pundits, players and reporters than by Ferguson himself. Ferguson even claimed that it was something of a myth, and that he only ever resorted to it when players talked back, estimating that it happened around six times in total during his 27 years as Manchester United manager.[15] Myth or not, the idea is now a common way to describe the approach of coaches (in football and other sports) who favour a "tough love" approach.

The concept has also made its way into the wider world, despite warnings from some quarters about the dangers of applying a method from the football changing rooms to other walks of life. When Ferguson retired in 2013 to universal acclaim and a flood of tributes, Simon Jenkins wrote in the *Guardian* that his *hairdryer treatment* wouldn't have the same effect in the world of politics, where simply shouting at the economy wouldn't do much to fix it.[16] This hasn't stopped political interviewers from adopting the tactic, and Irish journalist Vincent Browne was said to have favoured the more combative approach to interviewing, once reportedly giving the *hairdryer treatment* to an evasive senator on his current affairs show.[17] TV interviewer Jeremy Paxman was often described as giving the *hairdryer treatment* to politicians, including to both David Cameron and Ed Miliband during a live TV debate in the run-up to the 2015 UK general election.[18] More recently, in 2019, it was suggested that government Chief Advisor Dominic Cummings should be giving the *hairdryer treatment* to Conservative MP Jacob Rees-

Mogg for his bizarre decision to lounge across the benches of the House of Commons during a Parliamentary session.[19]

Ferguson's legacy (sporting and linguistic) is significant, and another example of his contribution to the vocabulary, albeit not one that has made it beyond the world of football, is the concept of *Fergie time*, which refers to any excessive amount of additional time added on at the end of a match. Such time is routinely added to account for injuries and other stoppages, but a well-established "fact" amongst football fans is that a disproportionate amount of time always seemed to be added on when Ferguson's Manchester United side were in need of a late goal to save a match. The idea originated during the 1992-1993 football season, when Manchester United scored a winning goal against Sheffield Wednesday in the 96th minute of the match. To be fair, the game had featured a lengthy stoppage as a result of an injury (to the referee!), but on plenty of other occasions during the following 20 years, opposing fans had cause to bemoan the excessive generosity of referees in adding time on to allow Manchester United to salvage or win games right at the death. In 2012 BBC Sport ran an analysis to see whether there was any reality to the myth, and found that there did seem to be more time added on when top teams (not just Manchester United) were losing at home compared to when they were winning.[20] In an interview in 2014, Ferguson himself did confess that he used to deliberately gesture toward his watch to get into the head of referees and encourage them to add extra time on when it was needed, so perhaps there was something in *Fergie time* after all.

Move the goalposts

To change the parameters or alter the rules whilst an event is still in progress.

Moving the goalposts can be attributed to any sport that uses goalposts, so we can take our pick from football, rugby, American football, ice hockey and many others. The imagery is clear, as to move the goalposts mid-game would be to put the opposition at a considerable disadvantage. The more metaphorical use of the phrase has the same meaning when applied to arguments, debates, applications or official processes, with an implication that something underhand has happened to handicap one participant or group.

An early written example of the phrase used in a very literal sense featured in a curious piece from *New Scientist* magazine in 1976.[21] An article entitled "Dislocated Goalposts" reported on the widespread belief that Kenyan football at the time was being unduly influenced by black magic. The Kenyan football authorities apparently believed that "95% of clubs were suspected of employing witchdoctors to help them win matches". Antics included the ability to make the ball disappear, freeze players on the spot, or even to *move the goalposts*. Belief in the supernatural influence over football was not restricted to Kenya, and the article goes on to report on Italian football club AC Milan apparently employing a Franciscan Father to maximise the likelihood of divine intervention, as well as someone nicknamed "The Magician of Peloro" who attempted to lift the "evil eye" from Sicilian club Messina FC at a curse-lifting ceremony. (To their credit, Messina FC didn't show up to take part.) Even in the UK, a reported 100-year curse placed on Birmingham City led manager Barry Fry to desperate lengths to end a winless run. In 1993, following curse-lifting advice from the traveller community, he relieved himself on the four corner flags (something he claimed was "not that easy"). An immediate change in fortunes made Fry a firm believer, even if no one else was.[22] More recently, and significantly less spookily, Swedish goalkeeper Kim Christensen was caught *moving the goalposts* by pushing them closer together before a match in 2009. The authorities reported this as the first time such a thing had happened in Swedish football, but Christensen apparently said that he had been given the tip by another goalkeeper and had done it in matches previously.[23] In other sports, such as ice hockey where goalposts can be moved inadvertently through contact by the players, rules exist specifically to outlaw such behaviour if done deliberately.

The Phrase Finder suggests that *move the goalposts* became popular in the UK during the 1980s and its figurative meaning can be traced back almost as far as the goings on in Kenya. Writer William Safire, well known for his "On Language" column in *The New York Times Magazine*, wrote about it in 1990, citing an example from 1978 when Albert Casey of American Airlines complained that people kept *"moving the goal posts"* when it came to the deregulation of airlines.[24] Regular uses can be observed from the 1980s onward, with notable examples recorded during debates in the British Parliament, lending support to William Safire's conclusion that this was originally a British term. However, an even earlier usage comes from an article in *Time* magazine in 1972, where the US government was accused of "trying to *move the goalposts*" in their efforts to meet employment targets. This example is cited by Idiomation, which also suggests that the use of the phrase in this way might indicate that it was already in common usage and likely originated sometime in the 1960s (and not necessarily in the UK).[25]

The phrase is a common one now, and the affront to fair play that it represents makes it an evocative image, especially when wealthier or more powerful players are *moving the goalposts* to make it even harder for poorer or less privileged groups. Jeremy Hobbs, then Executive Director of Oxfam International, suggested that this was exactly what was happening in 2011 in an article entitled *"Moving the Goal Posts"*. Global Aid targets, agreed in 2005, had been consistently missed by the countries supposed to be delivering financial aid, despite the poorer recipient countries holding up their end of the deal by tackling corruption and taking significant steps to better manage the aid they received. How did the countries respond? According to Hobbs, "Like a five-year-old losing a kick-around in the park. Rather than trying harder, they change the rules."[26] As Hobbs also points out, this highlights one of the other issues with *moving the goalposts*, which is the logical fallacy that any victory it leads to ultimately counts for much less (not that this seemed to bother Kim Christensen too much).

Park the bus

To set oneself up to defend a position at all costs.

In footballing terms, *parking the bus* means playing in an ultra-defensive fashion, with almost all players concentrating on defending their own goal rather than attacking the opposition one. The phrase is often attributed to Portuguese football manager José Mourinho, who has divided opinion and ruffled feathers ever since he entered English football in 2004. Following a match in September 2004 when Chelsea (the team he managed) drew 0-0 with Tottenham Hotspur, Mourinho criticised the defensive approach adopted by his opponents and told reporters, "As we say in Portugal, they brought the bus and they left the bus in front of the goal." Later that season, before the return fixture, he took the theme up again, saying, "We bring the bus this time. We are going to try to win but maybe we need to *park the bus*." People picked up on the idea and *parking the bus* became a common accusation when one team sets out to defend for their lives. Languagecaster, which aims to help people learn English through football related resources, lists an entry from 2008 where *parking the bus* is defined in these terms,[27] and the phrase is now a common expression in the vocabulary of football fans everywhere.

Despite being generally seen as a negative tactic, not everyone agrees that it is an approach to be condemned. For weaker teams, aiming to defend well and look for opportunities to counter-attack may be the best approach, if the alternative is to take on a technically more proficient opposition side at their own game and be played off the park. One blogger on Football Supernova in 2012 decried the "myth of *'parking the bus'*", reminding readers that football is as much about defence as attack, and pointing out the skill and organisation that such an approach actually requires.[28] Italian football, long-famed for the pride taken in solid and impassable defence, has its own term – "catenaccio", which translates as "door-bolt" – to describe a highly organised and effective defensive line. And whilst Mourinho may have started the trend of complaining about such a tactic in his opposition, he was certainly not afraid to employ it himself to good effect. In 2014, during his second stint in charge of Chelsea, he was accused by Liverpool manager Brendan Rodgers of an overly defensive approach. Rodgers, frustrated at his side's inability to break down the opposition, said afterward, "They *parked two buses,* rather than one", but since Chelsea won the match 2-0, Mourinho was probably none too concerned at the criticism.[29]

Like others in this chapter, *parking the bus* has also started to creep into use outside of football. One example relates to a budget speech made by Malusi Gigaba of the African National Congress in 2017. The speech was decidedly underwhelming, and one journalist suggested that Gigaba had "certainly *'parked the bus'* ahead of next year's crucial forecast", implying that the ANC were deliberately adopting a defensive approach for fear of making promises they couldn't keep.[30] An article from 2019 suggested that *parking the bus* was likely to become a common strategy for investors in times of economic uncertainty, further indicating a spread to the wider world. But the real evolution of *park the bus* has been within football, where people have begun to put their own stamp on the idea. As well as the obvious extension of parking two buses above, an academic article on the topic (using Brendan Rodgers' lament as its title) has explored the creative use of the metaphor, highlighting several uses where fans have added their own twists.[31] Journalists have gotten in on the act, such as one suggesting that when Mourinho became coach of Manchester United, "They did not so much as *park the bus* as throw the keys into the stand" against top opposition.[32] Another described how a plan by Scotland to thwart England in the 2019 FIFA Women's World Cup by *parking the bus* quickly fell apart, with "the windscreen smashed by Parris's penalty, [and] the high intensity and relentless press from the Lionesses enough to take the wheels off the bus."[33] So, like it or loathe it, *bus parking* is not about to disappear from football any time soon.

Squeaky bum time

A time of extreme nervousness and high tension.

Another phrase that can be attributed to Sir Alex Ferguson (see *The hairdryer treatment*, this chapter), *squeaky bum time* entered the vocabulary of football fans everywhere in 2003. That year, Ferguson's Manchester United were vying with rivals Arsenal for the English Premier League title, and he famously described the increasingly tense climax of the season as *"squeaky bum time"* during a television interview. The Phrase Finder website suggests that this refers to the noise made as those watching the game squirm in their seats. Plausible as this seems, an alternative is offered by Urban Dictionary, which claims that the phrase is "Old Glaswegian" and refers to being "on the verge of...", well, you can probably guess how that sentence ends.[34] Despite the lack of any evidence to support the "Old Glaswegian" part, it's worth noting that Alex Ferguson was born in Govan, part of the City of Glasgow, so it is not impossible that this was a familiar and colourful way to describe particularly stressful situations in that part of the world.

Plenty of examples provide a clear indication that for most people, the "squirming in the seats" allusion is not where the mind immediately goes. In a comment on the English Premier

League title race in early 2019, one writer suggested, "For Liverpool, it's *squeaky bum time* and [rival manager] Guardiola is more than willing to supply the laxatives."[35] Football legend and presenter Gary Lineker went one step further with a Tweet in 2016, during the run-in of a season in which Leicester City pulled off one of the upsets of all time by winning the English Premier League. His Tweet remarked that it was, "getting close to *squeaky bum time*", and went on to add: "From personal experience that can get very messy." This was a reference to the 1990 World Cup, when, during England's opening match and whilst suffering from a particularly bad case of upset stomach, Lineker, in his own words, "relaxed himself" on the pitch. At least he could laugh about it in 2016 (a mere quarter of a century later…).

A majority of modern uses do refer to football, but the phrase also appears in reference to cricket (specifically to the tense end of a close game) and rugby (referring to both a tense end to a season and the final period of a close game) with the same meaning. *Squeaky bum time* was even coined as the name of a podcast released by Radio New Zealand during the 2018 FIFA World Cup, suggesting that it has come a long way from its humble roots in working class Glasgow. The phrase has also made its way beyond the world of sport. Tech giants Apple were involved in two such situations in quick succession in 2016: first the EU vowed to end Ireland's "special tax status" with big companies and demanded that Apple fork out $14.5 billion in unpaid taxes, leading to *squeaky bum time* for the Irish economy,[36] then, a month later, one IT commentator declared "*squeaky bum time*" for Apple in response to falling sales.[37] Elsewhere, politics seems to have also emerged as a favoured domain for this particular phrase. Trevor Noah, the South African comedian and television host, did his best to import the phrase to the USA when he Tweeted, "I know Americans don't use this phrase but this is totally *squeaky bum time*" following

Trump's election in 2016. The UK Conservative Party has also suffered twice with the condition in recent times. During the 2017 general election, it was apparently "*squeaky bum time* at Conservative campaign headquarters", at the prospect of a Labour-Scottish National Party alliance. Some years previously, as his party's lead in the polls started to dwindle in the run-up to the 2010 general election, then Conservative leader David Cameron was asked whether it was "*squeaky bum time* for the Conservatives". His reply – that, "There's certainly nothing squeaking over here" – might not go down as one of the great political quips, but it wasn't bad for the spur of the moment.[38]

Take one for the team

To endure personal injury for the benefit of one's colleagues or teammates.

Taking one for the team seems to have emerged from baseball, in the context of a weaker batter deliberately allowing her/himself to be hit by the ball (if a batter is "hit by pitch", she or he is automatically allowed to advance to first base, thereby earning the team a potential run). The phrase is also common in football where a player may commit a deliberate foul and incur a yellow card rather than allow a potentially dangerous attack to develop, and is now in more common usage to mean "suffer something unpleasant for the greater good".

The Big Apple website lists the possible earliest use of the term in print from 1969, referring directly to a baseball game.[39] Several other uses are listed from throughout the 1970s, each with a fairly literal reference to a baseball game, but by 1980 there is an example from an article entitled "Bristol defends fight", where a reporter was asked to "*take one for the team*" and keep quiet about an "incident" that had apparently "stunned" players and coaches. Modern references to the practice in a range of sports are common, but no more so than in its more general, metaphorical sense. One such use (among many) came in an article reporting a fairly unsavoury incident during a high school American football match in Virginia in 2013. The Annandale Atoms reached half-time in the final match of their season, and the Marching Atoms (the school's band) took to the field to perform. Unfortunately, they overran, risking a penalty being imposed on the home team, since not restarting the game on time carries such a punishment in the rules of American Football. Knowing this, the crowd quickly turned on the poor musicians, demanding that they be removed, and a report of the incident asked whether it was "asking too much to *take one for the team*" and allow the band to finish their show.[40] In a very different sense, and demonstrating quite how extended the metaphor has become, a review of the ninth *Star Wars* film, released in 2019, declared that "the entire prequel trilogy is there to *take one for the team* and prevent *The Rise of Skywalker* from being the weakest of the nine".[41]

Returning to sport, the idea of *taking one for the team* is certainly one that divides opinion, usually based on which team is being benefited by the tactic. An incident early in 2020 prompted BBC Sport to ask just this, when it reported on the football match between arch-rivals Real Madrid and Atlético Madrid in the Spanish Super Cup final.[42] Ending 0-0 and deep into extra time, Atlético striker Álvaro Morata rushed through on goal, only to be hacked down by Real's Federico Valverde in an "exhibition of the dark arts" that prevented a possible goal, but got the Real player sent off in the process. Since his team went on to win the match on penalties, Valverde was hailed as a hero, named as man of the match, and even congratulated afterward by Atlético coach Diego Simeone (himself no stranger to the "whatever it takes to win" attitude). The article cites other famous examples, none more obvious than the actions of Uruguay striker Luis Suárez in his country's 2010 FIFA World Cup quarter final against Ghana. Suárez chose to suffer a red card and subsequent suspension by punching the ball off the line in the final seconds of the match to prevent a certain goal. His actions worked (depending on your perspective), when Ghana missed the resultant penalty with literally the last kick of the match, and Uruguay went on to win the subsequent penalty shootout. As the BBC article concludes, "Truly reprehensible/admirable stuff… depending on your point of view."

The world of sports is a rich source of catchphrases, clichés and, as we see, idioms aplenty. In particular, the big spectator sports – in the UK, cricket, football and horse racing; in the USA, baseball and American football – have contributed much in the way of reusable terminology. But it is also interesting to consider why some sports seem to be absent here. Despite its popularity around the world, phrases from rugby seem quite thin on the ground (to *kick something into touch*, meaning to shelve an idea or discussion, is about as close as it comes, although the idea of an *up and under* – a big kick forward followed by a charge forward by the team – seems like the kind of thing that could easily be appropriated). Plenty of other sports are similarly not represented, even when armies of fans would doubtless recognise allusions or references from a range of pursuits. Many people would understand phrases like *nine dart finish*, *147 break* or *bowling a 300*, which represent a perfect (and fairly uncommon) achievement in darts, snooker and ten-pin bowling respectively, but none have so far made it into the wider world. Perhaps as audiences continue to grow, these too might find their way into the language.

6

Doing it by the Book: Idioms from Modern Literature

Before movies and TV shows got in on the act, literature had been contributing turns of phrase to English for centuries. Linguist David Crystal suggested that no better example exists than the King James Bible, and explores the contribution of this work in terms of idioms and proverbs in his 2010 book *Begat: The King James Bible and the English Language*.[1] Another prolific source is Shakespeare, who is credited with inventing, popularising or providing a first written record of hundreds of words and phrases. Milton is said to have contributed more individual words,[2] but Shakespeare is a clear winner when it comes to phrases. Whilst there is no definitive record of these (some sources list over 150 examples), phrases that certainly appeared in Shakespeare plays and which are still in common usage today include *break the ice* (The Taming of the Shrew), *wear your heart on your sleeve* and *a foregone conclusion* (Othello), *too much of a good thing* and *forever and a day* (As You Like It), *be-all and end-all* and *one fell swoop* (Macbeth), and *dead as a doornail* (Henry VI Part II), to name but a handful.

Plenty of other writers have had their say, and notable contributions that are now a common part of everyday vocabulary include *Frankenstein's monster* (*Frankenstein*; Mary Shelley, published 1818), referring to something that becomes dangerous or harmful to those that created it; *Jekyll and Hyde* (*The Strange Case of Dr Jekyll and Mr Hyde*; Robert Louis Stevenson, published 1886), used to describe anyone with wildly different sides to their personality; a *scarlet letter* (from the novel of the same name by Nathaniel Hawthorne, published 1850), indicating a visible mark or sign to remind people of a past mistake; and *quixotic* people, being those who demonstrate a certain detachment from reality by *tilting at windmills* (*Don Quixote*; Miguel de Cervantes, published 1605).

Whilst none of these can reasonably be described as "modern", more recent authors can certainly lay claim to also influencing the language in profound ways. Lewis Carroll, writing in the 19th century, introduced the enduring *Alice's Adventures in Wonderland* (published 1865), which in turn contributed the idea of going *down the rabbit hole* (to enter into a confusing or unknown situation), as well as phrases like *grinning like a Cheshire Cat* (used to describe someone smiling from ear to ear) and *mad as a hatter* (completely mad; forever associated with the *Wonderland* character, but likely used by Carroll as an already well-known phrase).[3] Carroll also coined a number of individual words in his writings, often blending other words in order to do so: "chortle" is one example (a combination of "chuckle" and "snort"), and the very term "portmanteau word", referring to a word formed by combining two existing words, is also attributed to him.[4]

In the 20th century, George Orwell may be one of the more obvious contributors, with concepts from the novel *1984* (published 1949) such as *Room 101* (a room containing unspeakable horrors) and *Big Brother* (a totalitarian leader watching what everyone does at all times) entering the language and, subsequently, the world of television. Similarly, from another of Orwell's works, *Animal Farm* (published 1945), the maxim *four legs good, two legs bad* (used in the original novel to symbolise the distinction between animals and humans) and the self-contradicting commandment *all animals are equal, but some are more equal than others* will be familiar to many people. Both are examples of phrases that are sometimes used to comment on real-life instances of, in the first example, a dogmatic imbalance of power between two groups, and in the second, the abuse of both power and logic by those at the top claiming to be constrained by the same rules as those they oversee. Alongside these, J.R.R. Tolkien made his mark (no one had heard of *Hobbits* before 1937), as, more recently, did J.K. Rowling (who introduced us to *muggles, quidditch* and any number of fantastic beasts).

The examples in this chapter have all emerged as fairly common turns of phrase in modern English, even if (in some cases at least) their origins may not be particularly widely known.

All quiet on the Western Front

An indication that nothing is happening, often with an implication of stagnation or boredom.

A fairly straightforward one to start, *all quiet on the Western Front* is an established way of indicating that everything is calm, or that nothing is happening at the present time. The phrase originates from World War I, where the Western Front represented the main area of conflict, in particular of trench warfare. More specifically, the phrase was used as the English Translation of a German novel, *Im Westen Nichts Neues* or, literally "Nothing New in the West", published toward the end of the 1920s. (The book itself was published in 1929, but had been serialised in a German newspaper the previous year.) Written by Erich Maria Remarque, himself a survivor of the trenches, the novel was an instant success, sending a strong anti-war message through its vivid and harrowing account of the war that resonated with those who had lived through the conflict. Some have claimed it to be the first genuine international bestseller, and (in what has become time-honoured fashion) a Hollywood blockbuster soon followed (in 1930), released to widespread acclaim in the USA.

Elsewhere, the impact of the novel and film were very different. In Germany, the film in particular was seized upon by the burgeoning Nazi party as a threat to their ideology, even becoming "a proxy for Nazi rage" due to its lack of pro-German stance.[5] When the film was released in Germany, groups of Nazi Brownshirts led assaults on cinemas, disrupting screenings and attacking moviegoers (especially those identified as Jewish), and quickly leading the German board of film censors to ban the release. More was to follow, and when the Nazis came to power in 1933, *All Quiet on the Western Front* was amongst the many books that were condemned, banned and burned. Erich Remarque had already fled Germany by this point, and by the end of 1933 the Nazis had made it illegal for anyone to own a copy of the novel, or its sequel, *The Road Back*. The film (briefly re-released in a heavily edited form in 1931) was not fully available in Germany until 1952.

Such a turbulent beginning belies the modern use of *all quiet on the Western Front* as a fairly prosaic way to describe lack of activity or inaction. The phrase is also easily modified: *all quiet on the X front* is commonly used to indicate no particular developments in whatever topic is being talked about, as in examples like *"All quiet on the Brexit front"*,[6] to suggest a relative lack of activity around an otherwise newsworthy topic. Other modifications include the 1990s BBC comedy drama *All Quiet on the Preston Front*, and a punk/hardcore compilation LP chronicling the punk scene in California and Nevada in the early 1980s, entitled *Not So Quiet on the Western Front*. Such creative uses all suggest the fairly entrenched (no pun intended) nature of the phrase in modern English.

Brave new world

An era of hope and optimism as a result of changes or advancements in society (often used ironically).

Officially another of Shakespeare's contributions (appearing in a speech in Act V of *The Tempest*), *brave new world* is perhaps more widely associated with the dystopian novel of the same name by Aldous Huxley, published in 1932. The book presents a view of the future (dated in the 26th century) where the whole planet is governed by a World State, and society has been transformed through genetic modification, social engineering, hypnopaedia (sleep learning) and various forms of population control. The harmony of this world is disrupted when a "savage" from one of the reservations outside of the control of the World State is brought in to witness the *brave new world* for himself.

Commentators have suggested that Huxley (an established writer and satirist) primarily drew on the feeling between World Wars that technology was the answer to all of humanity's problems, intending to take the premise to its extreme to demonstrate how naïve it was. Parallels have often been drawn with an earlier work, *We*, by Russian author Yevgeny Zamyatin, which deals with similar themes. Huxley denied having read the book prior to writing *Brave New World*, and many have pointed out that fears regarding the advancement of technology were not uncommon at the time. By all accounts the reaction to the novel's release was mixed, with many people not enjoying the prediction that even a world free of poverty and suffering might still present plenty of problems for humanity. Writer Margaret Atwood, herself no stranger to painting a fairly bleak view of the future, pondered as much on the 75th anniversary of the novel, concluding that such questions explain why Huxley's work continues to hold such an important place in modern literature.[7] Various adaptations, including a TV series in 2020, have helped to keep the work alive over the years as well.

As an idiom, *brave new world* features in multiple online dictionaries, and both a face value and a more ironic or bleak meaning are generally listed. It either characterises an era full of hope and optimism for the future, or, more in line with the theme of the novel, describes a period where advances and developments that seem to have innumerable benefits have in fact made things worse in many ways. One 2015 article made just this point, that to use *brave new world* at face value was to miss the nuance of the "phrase of snark", where all is not as rosy as may first appear. Hence, it is not right to talk of a *brave new world* for cricket, streaming TV or airline companies (as people have done), but "if robots turn around and try to kill us all that would be a *brave new world* indeed."[8] One website offering writing tips cites several examples of *brave new world* in news headlines, pointing out that because of the negative connotations, sometimes such a choice may be less than appropriate.[9]

A survey of uses does suggest that more often than not the phrase is used with its slightly ironic or sinister connotations. A 2019 article on the age of disinformation suggested that, given its role in the misappropriation and misuse of online data, "Cambridge Analytica is the poster child for this *brave new world*."[10] Elsewhere, it's hard to tell whether the use of the phrase is intended to suggest more than the writer is explicitly saying. One report suggested that the choice of José Mourinho (see *Park the bus*, Chapter 5) as manager of Tottenham Hotspur in 2019 was a "*brave new world* for Tottenham".[11] Without knowing either this particular writer's opinion about Mourinho or the depth of literary knowledge being drawn on, it's hard to tell quite how the reference was intended.

Catch-22 / a Catch-22 situation

A situation where the desired outcome cannot be achieved due to the paradoxical nature of the rules.

Joseph Heller's most famous work, *Catch-22*, was first published in 1961, although Heller began planning the story and wrote the first chapter some years earlier. Often hailed as one of the greatest novels of the 20th century, *Catch-22* is a satire set during World War II. The story revolves around a Captain in the US Air Force, Yossarian, who gradually comes to the conclusion that he has more to fear from his own commanding officers than from the enemy, primarily because as he flies more and more combat missions, the number of completed missions required for a pilot to return home continues to increase (see also *Move the goalposts*, Chapter 5).

The title refers to a paradox laid out in the novel, typified by the idea that anyone who would willingly fly in highly dangerous combat missions was, by definition, crazy, and could therefore be grounded on medical grounds. However, to express such a desire would demonstrate a level of rational thought, thereby demonstrating that the pilot was, in fact, of perfectly sound mind, and could therefore be cleared to go on flying. The idea is repeated throughout the novel, each time exemplifying either a logical paradox, or the frustrating bureaucracy that seems to let the powers that be justify whatever course of action they choose. Toward the end of the book, this theme is developed to exemplify the abuse of power that the idea comes to represent.

Just like the significance of the number 42 (see *Life, the Universe and Everything*, this chapter), the choice of number seems to have relatively little importance in itself. Heller originally used the title Catch-18, which was changed after the publication of another war novel, *Mila 18*, and several other options were rejected before eventually *Catch-22* was chosen. Some have commented on the theme of repetition throughout the book (lots of things happen twice or more, and on publication some critics even pointed out the extent of this repetition, suggesting that it was sloppy writing). Heller himself suggested that the idea wouldn't translate into other languages, and even relayed a story of a Finnish translator who contacted him asking for clarification of "what means *Catch-22*?" As Heller said, "I suspect the book lost a great deal in its Finnish translation."[12]

Examples of *Catch-22 situations* abound in modern life. On the 50th anniversary of the book's publication, one journalist simply wrote, "everybody knows what a *Catch-22* is".[13] It seems like a fairly accurate claim, and most online dictionaries list it as a classic impossible situation, where the solution cannot be achieved because of the nature of the condition. Issues surrounding finance and housing have been described in such terms, such as the idea that making house prices more affordable might require house prices to be lowered, which would be such an unpopular move that it would likely make sure that house prices stayed high. In other words, "we have a *Catch-22*: action must be seen to be taken on the housing crisis, but on no account should this action result in lower house prices."[14] The same idea was applied to the "Brexit *Catch-22*" in 2019, where the make-up of the UK Parliament meant that no decision could be made as to the best course of action because no one position could command enough votes to pass.[15] Psychological *Catch-22s* are apparently also common, since "human psychology is replete with conflict, contradiction, and paradox."[16] It's just lucky that we've got such a good term to describe it when it happens.

Life, the Universe and Everything

A collection of unspecified and miscellaneous topics.

Life, the Universe and Everything is a recurring idea throughout *The Hitchhiker's Guide to the Galaxy*, a comedy science fiction series created by English writer Douglas Adams. It has appeared in numerous formats, starting life as a radio series which ran from 1978 to 1980 on BBC Radio 4. A novel followed in 1979, adapting most of the first radio series, with several other books, a TV adaptation, video game and movie to carry on the story in the decades to follow. Adams undertook extensive rewrites for each adaptation, but the same basic plot and cast of memorable characters remains relatively consistent. The story broadly follows Arthur Dent, last surviving human after the Earth is destroyed to make way for a hyperspace bypass, and his travelling companion Ford Prefect, an alien writer and field researcher (for the titular *Guide*) who happened to be stationed on Earth at the time of its destruction. The pair escape Earth immediately prior to its demolition, precipitating the adventures that follow. *The Hitchhiker's Guide* acts as an overarching title for the series and as a plot device, as it also comes in useful as a source of information for intrepid adventurers wanting to explore the reaches of space.

The phrase *Life, the Universe and Everything* appears both as the title of the third novel and as an important plot point throughout all versions of the story. As a precursor to the events of the series, a group of super-intelligent beings demand to know the answer to the most important question of all: the meaning of *Life, The Universe, and Everything*. To achieve this, they construct a supercomputer whose sole purpose is to figure out the answer. After seven and a half million years of computation, the computer returns the answer – 42 – pointing out that the answer seems to make no sense because it was not asked the right question.

The phrase has now taken on a more general meaning akin to "anything and everything", in particular in the context of Internet forums. Something labelled as such is a section for general or off-topic discussions. One of the more notable examples was a section on long-standing video game site GameFAQs, which includes a social message board entitled *Life, the Universe and Everything* (or LUE for short). Originally intended for genuine philosophical discussion, the forum quickly degenerated into less savoury areas, with "memes, crude conversations, and irreverent discussion where nothing was off limits".[17]

References to 42 as the answer to the meaning of life also abound in both technology and popular culture. It provides a common theme in software and Internet development, where programmers have a habit of weaving the number into their output in a variety of ways, as well as cropping up from time to time in TV shows (predictably, science fiction in particular). The Allen Telescope Array, focused on searching for extraterrestrial life, originally included 42 antennae in its phase one construction, apparently in homage to the idea. Douglas Adams was often quizzed as to the relevance of the choice of number, and although various theories have been proposed,

Adams himself was often quoted as saying that he simply picked a number at random, aiming for something simple that he thought represented a funny number. He explained his choice on an Internet discussion forum in 1993, saying, "It had to be a number, an ordinary, smallish number, and I chose that one." This hasn't stopped fans, mathematicians and inquiring minds everywhere looking for deeper meaning, including the observation that 42 also crops up with suspicious regularity in the works of Lewis Carroll.

Yet another contribution from *The Hitchhiker's Guide* that certainly deserves wider use is the idea that *knowing where your towel is* should be taken as a sign that a person is entirely in control and prepared for any situation. In the original novel (modelled on similar wording in the radio series), a towel is described as being amongst the most useful items an interstellar traveller can carry, and the text goes on to list a number of innovative and potentially life-saving uses for such an article. Fans have immortalised the towel as a tribute to Douglas Adams and the *Hitchhiker's* universe by celebrating Towel Day on the 25th May every year since 2001 (the year of Adams' death). On this day, fans across the universe carry a towel with them to mark the occasion, presumably, in the process, being ready for anything the day may throw at them.[18] In sympathy with this (and in particular if you don't *know where your towel is*), one final phrase from *The Hitchhiker's Guide* (according to the story, printed in large letters on the cover of the book) was described by science fiction behemoth Arthur C. Clarke as "The best advice" for all of humankind: *don't panic!*[19]

No shit, Sherlock

A sarcastic exclamation used to indicate that someone has stated something obvious.

Auguste Dupin, created by mystery writer Edgar Allan Poe, is widely considered to be literature's first fictional detective, although he is considerably less well-known than "the world's most famous literary detective", Sherlock Holmes.[20] Often described as the prototype for the modern criminal investigator, Holmes appeared in four novels and 56 short stories written by Arthur Conan Doyle, although multiple other authors have adapted the characters in other works over the years. Radio, TV and movies have also been fertile ground for adaptations, and *The Guinness Book of Records* (at least as of 2012) lists Sherlock Holmes as having been portrayed more times than any other human character in movie history (254), with only Dracula (272) beating him to the title of most portrayed literary character overall.[21]

The origin of *no shit, Sherlock* is therefore pretty unequivocal. The allusion is to the great investigator, with the highly sarcastic implication that whatever has been said or concluded hardly required the skills of a master consulting detective. Identifying when the idiom actually first emerged, however, is a little trickier. Know Your Meme cites one of the first uses in popular culture in the movie *Little Shop of Horrors* (1986), but suggests that the phrase itself dates to sometime around the 1940s or 1950s. Discussions of the origin online do feature claims that the phrase was in common usage in 1950s USA, and possibly as early as the 1930s. Certainly people began using Sherlock Holmes to denote "master detective" in the 1920s, and one example from *Time* magazine (about a fire at the home of Arthur Conan Doyle) in 1929 even used it in a comparable sense, stating that "no Sherlock Holmes was needed to detect the cause."[22] The earliest written uses of *no shit, Sherlock* seem to come from the 1970s, and one reason for the lack of evidence of earlier usage is the fact that the phrase lends itself more to spoken interaction than written. The use of an obscenity probably also meant that it was less likely to be recorded in many texts.

A slightly cleaner version exists in the alternative phrase, *thank you, Captain Obvious*, with both serving as bywords for "stating the obvious". In the UK, TV viewers may be familiar with the character from accommodation booking website Hotels. com, which launched a campaign featuring *Captain Obvious* in 2014 based on the idea that use of the site to take advantage of a good deal is such an obvious choice as to make it a no-brainer. In the USA, however, the character has a much more developed backstory, and is often portrayed as a superhero with the special power of making extremely self-evident statements. The precise origins of Captain Obvious are unclear (some sources date this to a skit first performed by a comedy troupe in the late 1980s[23]), although it seems to have entered US slang by the early 1990s and shows a steady increase in usage from that point onward. In what may be an unrelated twist, Google Books provides a photograph from the *Chemical Warfare Bulletin*, published in 1926, listing names of members of the 302nd Gas Regiment and what seem to be "affectionate" nicknames. The nickname provided for one Captain Firebaugh is *Captain Obvious*, suggesting that the joke may have been around for quite a while before it really made its way into more common use.[24]

No shit, Sherlock, meanwhile, has inspired a range of modern uses, including the sub-reddit of the same name featuring a collection of news headlines that "make you go, '*no shit, Sherlock*'". Particularly good examples are a story posted in 2015 about a lion (Cecil) and his brother, who the sub-editor felt the need to specify "is also a lion", and a Tweet from the History Channel in 2017 suggesting that there may have been "a dark underside to the Nazi regime." Finally, in a re-literalisation of the phrase, *No Shit Sherlock* also featured as the name of a brand of scented lavatory mist, designed "For crime scenes of all types and sizes." Conan Doyle would undoubtedly have been very proud.

Screw the pooch
To make a total mess of things.

Whilst not the origin of the phrase, general consensus is that *screw the pooch*, meaning to make an almighty and often terminal mess of things, was popularised by the 1979 Tom Wolfe book *The Right Stuff*, along with its subsequent film adaptation. Wolfe became fascinated by the early days of the US space race, in particular what would motivate people to undertake the very dangerous job of attempting to fly into space. His book focused on the personal lives of the test pilots who formed Project Mercury, or the first operational manned US space-flight program. *Screwed the pooch* is used in the book to refer to an error leading to the loss of a space capsule (an incident involving pilot Virgil "Gus" Grissom that has been disputed ever since).[25] Given the extensive work done by Wolfe in researching the book, it's a fair assumption that the phrase was an authentic part of NASA jargon, and most sources confirm that it was indeed established military slang by the time *The Right Stuff* introduced it to the world.

How it made its way there, however, is a little more debatable. Sources such as Word Origins suggest that *screw the pooch* is a cleaned-up version of the original "fuck the dog", used in military circles since at least the 1930s.[26] Even earlier variations in the form of "feed the dog" have been reported, appearing in print as early as 1918, but with a slightly different meaning. Feeding the dog apparently described the supposed activities of a soldier who was killing time until orders came in, whilst "fucking the dog" could also be used to mean wasting time or slacking. Around the time of World War II, this more explicit version seemed to take on an additional meaning of "make a blunder", and from there came the more family-friendly softening to *screw the pooch*. One article suggests that the move from here to the halls of NASA may be directly attributed to John Rawlings, who in the spring of 1950 was an architecture student sharing a room with fellow student Jack May. May apparently warned his roommate that he was in danger of messing up his studies by procrastinating over a project he had to complete, and warned that Rawlings was "fucking the dog". Taken to task over his "vulgar and coarse" language, May came back with: "Is this better? You are *screwing the pooch*." Rawlings is reported to have howled with laughter, and since he went on to enlist in the Air Force and subsequently work as part of a team designing prototype spacesuits in the years before NASA began its work on manned space missions, it seems like an entirely plausible (if unverifiable) origin story.[27]

The usage of *screw the pooch* certainly spikes from around 1980 onward, confirming the role of *The Right Stuff* in introducing it to a wider audience, and the phrase is predominantly part of American rather than British English (as, for that matter, is the habit of calling dogs "pooches"). Uses in all walks of life reflect the sense of "making a terrible (often irreversible) mistake", including accusations that the US Navy *screwed the pooch* in shooting down an Iranian passenger flight (killing close to 300 people) in 1988,[28] and, in slightly less serious terms, that TV show *Game of Thrones* had *screwed the pooch* with some of its storyline choices.[29] We might even consider *the right stuff* – meaning "the required qualities for a specific job" – to be an idiom in its own right, and certainly this was the sense in which Wolfe was using it when he chose it as the title of his book. The origins go much further back (according to Word Origins, as far as the 18th century in printed records, so perhaps even further back than that in broader use)[30] but, just as with *screw the pooch*, many have claimed that *the right stuff* will be forever linked with Wolfe's work.

Sophie's choice

An impossible or extremely difficult decision with negative outcomes whatever choice is made.

As well known for the movie adaptation as the original novel, *Sophie's choice* represents a situation where a decision between two alternatives must be made, but where both outcomes are equally undesirable and damaging. The choice referred to in the title was that forced on Sophie, a Polish Catholic who was sent to the Auschwitz concentration camp by the Nazis during World War II. Upon arrival, Sophie was forced to decide which of her two children should be sent to die immediately in the gas chambers, and which would be allowed to continue to live in the camp. Sophie chose to sacrifice her eight-year-old daughter, in the hope that her son would be taken and raised as a German child, and is wracked with guilt over the decision throughout the story.

The novel, published in 1979, was controversial for many reasons, not least for its portrayal of a non-Jewish victim of the Holocaust. Author William Styron claimed that his intention was to acknowledge the atrocities perpetrated on Jews, but to also highlight similar acts of brutality against non-Jews (in particular Slavs and Christians). Significant backlash followed as a result, and has continued to be a point of contention ever since, although this did not stop the movie adaptation from enjoying critical and commercial success, including a Best Actress Oscar for Meryl Streep in the title role. The story was even adapted into an opera in 2002, despite some misgivings at the time about the suitability of the subject matter for such a medium.[31]

Controversy aside, most people now recognise *Sophie's choice* as an established idiom, and it has good company in English. Phrases with similar, albeit less sinister, associations are common (*between a rock and a hard place, between the devil and the deep blue sea, a no-win situation, the lesser of two evils*). Sometimes considered in the same bracket, *Hobson's choice* exemplifies a related but distinct kind of dilemma: where the choice is between what is on offer or nothing at all. Whilst not a modern idiom itself (it dates from at least the 17th century, and is said to relate to horse owner Thomas Hobson who offered customers wanting to hire one of his horses the choice of the one nearest the door or nothing), a play of the same name first performed in 1915 and numerous film adaptations have helped to keep the phrase in relatively common use.

Despite the deeply heart-wrenching nature of the original *Sophie's choice*, modern uses tend to relate to important, if not exactly life-and-death, situations. Some compared the 2016 presidential election, with the option of voting for Hillary Clinton or Donald Trump, to "a political version of a tragic *Sophie's choice*".[32] In the UK, the same was said of the 2019 Conservative Party leadership competition, with the country "faced with the prospect of either the most incompetent foreign secretary in history or the most incompetent health secretary in history becoming prime minister… quite the *Sophie's Choice*. Or Alien v Predator: whoever wins we lose."[33] Others have (hopefully with at least a hint of irony) diluted the horror implied by *Sophie's choice* quite a long way from the original. One writer suggested that the childhood decision of whether to spend her Christmas money on a Super NES or a Sega Genesis (or Megadrive as it was known in the UK) "seemed like a Sophie's Choice to a middle-class 10-year-old."[34] Another described the need to decide which of the Disney films *Frozen* or *Moana* had the better soundtrack as "like *Sophie's choice*".[35] And if these are the worst dilemmas we face in our lives, we can count ourselves pretty lucky.

Walter Mitty / a Walter Mitty personality

A daydreamer; someone who indulges in imagined flights of fancy regarding personal triumph.

Walter Mitty began his life in a short story – The Secret Life of *Walter Mitty* – first published in 1939. The title character is presented as an absent-minded and mild-mannered individual who, in the course of driving his wife into town to complete some errands, engages in a series of exciting daydreams. Each fantasy places him as a hero in a series of thrilling adventures – piloting a hydroplane through a ferocious storm, performing emergency surgery, facing trial as a deadly assassin, and volunteering to single-handedly fly a bomber into enemy territory – culminating in him standing smoking against a wall, which in his head he transforms into a noble end before a firing squad. The contrast between the humdrum nature of his everyday life and the adventures he imagines for himself have given rise to the description of people who indulge in such fantasies as *Walter Mitty* characters or personalities. Such a label is especially applied to people perceived to have delusions of grandeur that cannot possibly match the actual details of their relatively mundane lives. James Thurber, who created the character, enjoyed considerable success as a writer, despite suffering a childhood accident (his brother shot him in the eye with an arrow) that left him with around two-fifths of his vision. Some have commented that this may have contributed to Thurber's vivid imagination, even including a suggestion that he may have suffered from a neurological condition that causes hallucinations in blind people. This, it has been claimed, explains his tendency to write characters who, although physically unimposing and often put-upon, had a tendency to escape from real life via their fantasies. *Walter Mitty* is the obvious prime example of this, but several of Thurber's other characters show a similar habit, lending some weight to the theory (or at least confirming Thurber's enjoyment of a good daydream).

The Secret Life of *Walter Mitty* has twice been (loosely) adapted into a movie of the same name – in 1947 and more recently in 2013 – helping to keep the image of the hapless dreamer alive and well in modern culture. In the UK, the term gained widespread recognition in 2003 when it was used in relation to David Kelly, a Ministry of Defence weapons expert who caused controversy with off-the-record remarks made about the "sexed-up" nature of the dossier used by the British Government to justify the invasion of Iraq. In the furore that followed, some government sources were quick to attempt to discredit his views by branding him a *Walter Mitty* character and Kelly tragically took his own life. The outcry that followed such an accusation (levelled as it was against a UN adviser on biological warfare, so hardly someone with ideas above his station) led to an immediate climbdown, with government spokesman Tom Kelly (no relation) apologising "unreservedly" for the slight.[36]

Whilst the term does crop up from time to time when individuals are exposed as fantasists, one particular area where *Walter Mitty* is applied is the world of military service, where it is used as a label for individuals who lay claim to a heroic past that did not in fact exist. Whilst tall tales and the odd exaggeration here and there are harmless enough on their own, some take the deception so far as to join in parades or other military events decked out in medals that have been bought online rather than earned, incurring the wrath of genuine veterans in the process.[37] Anyone tempted to do the same should beware: the *Walter Mitty* Hunters Club exists to track down and expose such practices, with the press just waiting to pounce on anyone caught out as a "Walt".

Works of literature have contributed phrases in various ways, with titles, ideas and characters all settling in the wider consciousness. One final example of a phrase to enter common usage (even if it stretches the definition of "modern" a bit) is *swings and roundabouts*, meaning "good and bad things even out over time", which may date as far back as the early 1900s. The idea appears in a poem published in 1912 entitled *Roundabouts and Swings* by Patrick Reginald Chalmers, about the fluctuating fortunes of a travelling salesman, but an even earlier usage comes in the 1906 P.G. Wodehouse novel, *Love Among the Chickens*. Here, one character, musing on the ups and downs of life, says, "What we lose on the swings, we make up on the roundabouts", summing up the modern (and particularly

British) use of the phrase. Some sources go even further back, citing use of *swings and roundabouts* in a British Parliamentary Debate from 1895, where it was used as an established saying amongst costermongers (or street salesmen). It just goes to show that even when we have the records, we can sometimes never be quite sure where a phrase has come from. Thankfully, even in an age dominated by online content, streaming services and TV and movies on demand, books and the joy of reading show no signs of dying out, so hopefully literature has many a modern idiom to contribute yet.

7

The Best of the Rest

The phrases in this chapter can't be traced to specific TV shows or movies, or to Internet crazes, sporting references or books, but they have made it into our vocabulary nonetheless. For some, there are clear historical events, or at least developments that seem to have introduced an idea for the first time. For others, the phrase seems simply to have sprung into life at some point along the way, without a clear origin but with some clues as to how it was first coined. Regardless of exactly why, all are now firmly established in modern English (to a greater or lesser degree), and provide a range of useful phrases to round off our collection.

Dead cat strategy

To make a shocking or unpleasant announcement as a way of distracting from other issues.

The *dead cat strategy* – sometimes referred to as *throwing a dead cat on the table* or simply *dead catting* – is a tactic that has been employed by politicians in the 21st century as a way of distracting from otherwise unpleasant or potentially damaging news. Boris Johnson, Mayor of London at the time, outlined the strategy in a 2013 article on the subject of a proposed cap on bonuses in the banking sector. Decrying this as a cynical attempt by the EU to divert attention from economic turmoil all over the continent, Johnson described how the point of producing a *dead cat* was not to appal or disgust people, but simply to distract them. He went on to explain: "The key point, says my Australian friend, is that everyone will shout 'Jeez, mate, there's *a dead cat* on the table!'; in other words they will be talking about *the dead cat*, the thing you want them to talk about, and they will not be talking about the issue that has been causing you so much grief."[1] The "Australian friend" in question is Lynton Crosby, a political strategist generally credited with inventing the move (or at least coining the phrase). Crosby first managed election campaigns for the UK Conservative Party in 2005, later contributing to both the surprise majority in 2015 and the lost majority in 2017. He also masterminded Boris Johnson's successful London Mayoral campaigns in 2008 and 2012, which may explain Johnson's familiarity with *dead cats*.

Whilst a first use of either the phrase or the strategy is hard to pinpoint (it's a fair bet that politicians have been distracting people from unwelcome or uncomfortable attention for as long as there have been politicians), many see its pivotal use in the 2015 UK general election as the point that both sunk the Labour Party that year, and cemented the *dead cat* as a legitimate (or at least successful) political gambit. As Labour began to gain traction in the polls, Defence Secretary at the time, Michael Fallon, launched a vicious and fairly unforeseen attack on Labour Leader, Ed Miliband, accusing him of being "willing to stab the United Kingdom in the back to become Prime Minister."[2] The tactic worked, and, even if some claim that it was just the latest in a long line of *dead cats* employed by the Tories during the campaign, it is often seen as the moment that won them the election that year. Clearly fans of the "if it ain't broke..." approach, the Conservative Party was accused of using *dead cats* fairly liberally in the 2019 UK general election too, even if some felt that by then the whole thing had something of an air of crying wolf about it, or as one writer put it, "if everything is a *dead cat*, nothing is."[3]

Predictably, given the way US politics has played out since 2016, *dead cats* have also made their way to America, with Donald Trump accused of throwing them around whenever needed,[4] and presumably when "fake news" just doesn't cut it (see also *Collateral knowledge / collateral information*, Chapter 4).

More established in the USA is the idea that a good war can solve a multitude of problems at home, and the related idea of the "rally round the flag" effect (first proposed by political scientist John Mueller in 1970) describes just this. Here, a high profile international conflict not only provides a good distraction, but also a temporary upturn in approval for a sitting president. In this sense, another modern phrase, similar in form to the *dead cat strategy* but otherwise unrelated, is the idea of a *dead cat bounce*. More often applied in the world of finance, the *dead cat bounce* is a temporary recovery in share prices during a period when they are otherwise descending rapidly (the fairly grim logic being that even a dead cat bounces if it falls from a great enough height).[5] The charming expression is said to have emerged in the 1980s, with a 1985 article in the *Financial Times* quoting a city trader who described "what we call a '*dead cat bounce*'". The phrasing strongly suggests that this was already a well-established idea in the world of finance, and it is now well and truly a part of economic vocabulary. The idiom was also highlighted as "gaining currency in political circles" in 2016, describing a brief upturn in polls that are otherwise plummeting.[6] So whether they're on the table or falling from them, it seems that cats may have more of a role to play in politics than people might think.

Drink the Kool-Aid

To show absolute devotion to a person, idea or cause.

Kool-Aid may only be familiar to many in the UK through references on US television, but it has been a popular and successful brand since its invention in the 1920s. The product itself is a fairly innocuous type of fruit-flavoured drink, but its more sinister associations date back to the Jonestown massacre in 1978, when over 900 people died as a result of a mass poisoning, with Kool-Aid the alleged method of delivery. The massacre was an infamous chapter in the history of The

Peoples Temple of the Disciples of Christ, a religious movement formed in the USA in the 1950s. During the next two decades, its founder, Jim Jones, built a following that encompassed (by best estimates) up to 5,000 members. In 1974, Jones leased land in Guyana, South America, with the intention of building a socialist commune as a sanctuary from what some members saw as an increasingly unpleasant political climate in the USA, but others in the wider world saw as Jones fleeing the attention that his activities were receiving from media and law enforcement. Jones moved to the settlement – informally known as "Jonestown" – and by late 1978 close to 1,000 followers had joined him. In response to allegations of human rights abuses, in November 1978 US Congressman Leo Ryan visited the commune, where a number of Temple members indicated their desire to return home. They attempted to board a flight back to the USA, but Temple security guards opened fire, killing five people (including Ryan). That evening, Jones prepared a concoction of fruit drink laced with cyanide, leading to the deaths of 918 followers – including around 300 children – who ingested the mixture. According to reports, some may have done so willingly to commit suicide, but many were forced to drink or were injected with poison.

References to the incident began soon after, with American writer Allen Ginsberg reported as saying that "[we are] being told by our leaders to *drink the Kool-Aid* of nuclear power" during a speech in 1981.[7] Academic Rebecca Moore wrote a paper on the history of the phrase in 2002,[8] identifying common uses of *drinking the Kool-Aid*, including a 1982 comment on Ronald Reagan's economic policy, which "administers *Kool-Aid* to the poor, the deprived and the unemployed". Moore summarises other negative uses of the phrase that fall into two broad categories: relating to other cult-related incidents or tragedies (including the September 11th attacks, where many commentators compared the cult-like leadership and control employed by Osama Bin Laden with that demonstrated by Jones 25 years previously); and describing political contexts, for example during an energy crisis in California in 2001, when Democrat senator Nancy Pelosi described Republicans as "lining up to *drink Kool-Aid*" by voting to reject a cap to rates (thereby willingly and knowingly committing political suicide). More recently, *drinking the Kool-Aid* became a common trope during the 2016 US election, where the phrase was used to criticise followers (on both sides) for their perceived blind allegiance to their respective candidates.[9] In contrast, the phrase can have positive as well as negative connotations. In the world of business, to *drink the Kool-Aid* is often used to indicate wholehearted acceptance of an idea, belief or philosophy, often implying a leap of faith of some kind. The tech world seems to have been a particularly fertile context here, and Rebecca Moore cites the example of Bill Gates, who inspired huge levels of commitment from employees thanks to his vision of how Microsoft products could change the world for the better. Other tech companies embrace the idea that *drinking the Kool-Aid* can be a good thing, if employees or computer users get behind an idea and embrace it in a wholehearted way.

Some have objected to the use of the phrase on the grounds that it is insensitive, and that it trivialises and even misrepresents the people who lost their lives in the original Jonestown tragedy. Others have objected more on grounds of accuracy, since there seems to be ample evidence that rather than Kool-Aid, the cheaper alternative Flavor Aid was used in Jonestown. One writer on the topic of business ethics also highlighted the reputational damage that such a mis-association might bring, adding that to insist on accuracy "does the Flavor Aid folks no favours either".[10] Despite these objections, the phrase shows no signs of fading away, and was even crowned "the single most annoying example of business jargon" by *Forbes* in 2012.[11]

Drop the mic / mic drop

An expression of triumph at the end of a speech or performance; an impressive action that has a show-stopping effect.

Dropping the mic is an action by a performer to signal that what had been said or done is so impressive that no follow-up or response is required, or would even be worth listening to. The action is often noted as having been common in 1980s hip hop, particularly in rap battles, where success was marked by a performer ostentatiously *dropping the mic* to the floor. Whilst earlier examples do exist (notably, Judy Garland nonchalantly tossed away her microphone as she walked off stage after performing on *The Ed Sullivan Show* in 1965), the triumphalist air that the gesture now represents only emerged later on, also appearing in stand-up comedy. Eddie Murphy is acknowledged as one of the earliest *mic droppers* (during a live show in 1983, and in the 1988 movie *Coming to America*, as lead singer of soul band Sexual Chocolate). Chris Rock later followed suit, adopting the *mic drop* as a trademark way to end a successful set.

The idea really took off in 2012, when Barack Obama *dropped the mic* during an appearance on US talk show *Late Night with Jimmy Fallon*. Obama, along with Fallon and house band The Roots, "slow jammed the news" as a way of announcing that he intended to ask Congress to freeze interest rates on student loans. At the end of the performance he tentatively *dropped the mic* to the floor, to rapturous applause. The Internet loved it, and the phrase quickly took off. In a history of the *mic drop*, writer Forrest Wickman suggested that this was also due in no small part to *Saturday Night Live*, who had already featured Obama *dropping the mic* in earlier sketches, but who subsequently incorporated it into a parody of the presidential debate between Obama and Mitt Romney in October 2012.[12] Obama himself repeated the action in a speech at the White House Correspondents' Dinner in April 2016, ending his address by saying, "Obama Out," and *dropping the mic* (much more authoritatively than the first time).

Around the same time the Obamas traded figurative *mic drops* with Prince Harry during a promotional video for the Invictus Games, held in Florida later that year.

The idea is now firmly embedded in Internet culture, and the expression is often accompanied by the mimed gesture, if not an actual physical microphone. *Mic drop* joined the Oxford online dictionary in 2013, and both TV Tropes and Know Your Meme have entries to catalogue famous examples. The phrase has been applied retrospectively, for example to Ronald Reagan's *mic drop* moment during the 1984 presidential debates that is widely thought to have helped win him the US election that year.[13] Google even got in on the act when, on April Fool's Day 2016, it added a comical *"Mic Drop"* feature to Gmail allowing users to respond to an email with an animation of a cartoon Minion *dropping a mic*, as a way of shutting down an email thread. After a flurry of complaints (people inadvertently used the feature to send actual emails), the feature was rapidly removed, as Google acknowledged that it "caused more headaches than laughs".[14] Returning to its roots, *Drop the Mic* also became the title of a rap-battle themed US TV show – a spin-off of a segment from *The Late Late Show with James Corden* – where celebrities trade lyrical barbs in an effort to win votes from the studio audience. As of the end of the third season in 2019, Barack Obama is yet to take part.

Friends with benefits

Friends who regularly engage in sexual activity with one another without considering themselves to be in a committed relationship.

21st century dating may have been transformed by the advent of online dating and "hook up" apps, so much so that the idea of "swiping left/right" to show your approval or disapproval may even be a candidate for a modern idiom in itself. But, according to some, even better than the idea of meeting strangers for companionship and perhaps a bit more, is the idea of *friends with benefits*: a no strings attached sexual relationship with a close friend, where both partners know that emotional commitment is not part of the deal. If lifestyle websites are to be believed, the world is apparently full of people enjoying such a situation, although many are quick to point out that things don't always work out for the best.[15]

Various online sources suggest that a possible first usage comes from the Alanis Morissette song *Head Over Feet*, which appeared on the 1995 album *Jagged Little Pill*, later released as a single in 1996. The song includes reference to the phrase, although since the rest of the lyrics focus on the fact that the partners in the relationship being described are best friends as well as lovers, the rather casual sense of the phrase certainly was not apparent. It's unclear exactly when the shift from being-friends-as-well-as-lovers to sleeping-with-someone-without any-of-the-emotional-responsibility happened, but *friends with benefits* does show a slow increase from the mid-1990s, with an upsurge in the first decade of the 21st century. Certainly the use of the phrase as the title in several (unrelated) releases attests to its place as an established idea: an independent film entitled *Friends (With Benefits)* in 2009 (changed from the film's original and presumably less marketable title of "Fuck Buddies"); a 2011 romantic comedy *Friends with Benefits* starring Justin Timberlake and Mila Kunis; a short-lived 2011 US sitcom using the same title; the film *No Strings Attached* starring Natalie Portman and Ashton Kutcher, made under the working title *Friends with Benefits*; and several books in the "Romance" genre, as well as one variation on a theme in the novel *Friends Without Benefits: An Unrequited Love Romance*.

Despite the tendency of such arrangements to work out for the best in Hollywood movies, one study in 2015 suggested that only around 15% of *friends with benefits* situations develop into serious relationships. Much more likely is that one year on from entering into such an arrangement, the friends in question will have nothing more to do with each other.[16] As if to prove the myth, lifestyle magazines routinely warn against the pitfalls, highlighting the emotional complexities and boundaries that can so easily become blurred. The *Huffington Post* decried it as "The biggest lie in modern dating",[17] while *Psychology Today*, *Cosmopolitan* and *GQ* (amongst many others) all offer advice on how to make being *friends with benefits* work. A common theme: prioritising the friends part, making sure that the other things you would normally do with your friends don't get pushed to the background, and most importantly, picking the right friend!

Go postal
To become extremely, uncontrollably angry, often reacting in a violent way.

Acts of violence involving the mass, often indiscriminate shooting of innocent people have become sadly familiar in the 21st century. But such things are not new, and in the 1990s the term *going postal* was coined to reflect the perception that a high number of such acts were perpetrated by disgruntled or stressed-out workers at the United States Postal Service (USPS). The first attested use of the phrase, according to several different sources, was in an article from the *St. Petersburg Times* (St. Petersburg, Florida, rather than the Russian city) in December 1993. The article, entitled, "Violence at work tied to loss of esteem", stated that "The US Postal Service [...] has seen so many outbursts that in some circles excessive stress is known as *'going postal'*."[18] It goes on to clarify that the term is not one that the USPS approved of, and that the service had made (unspecified) attempts to stop people from using it. A second usage followed later that month, with the *Los Angeles Times* review of the year claiming that the rise of deadly mass shootings in the USA had given the English language a new term, with people "referring to shooting up the office as *'going postal'*."[19]

It's unclear how justified the USPS were in objecting to the use of the term. Incidents involving postal workers committing acts of gun violence at work date back to 1970, and between then and *going postal* entering the language in 1993, approximately 15 separate incidents took place at or were related to postal systems or premises. To try to settle the issue, a report commissioned by the Postmaster General published its findings in August 2000, concluding that "'*going postal*' is a myth, a bad rap. Postal workers are no more likely to physically assault, sexually harass, or verbally abuse their co-workers than employees in the national workforce." In addition, the risk of postal workers being victims of a homicide at work was around one-third that of the rest of the US workforce (of the 6,719 workplace homicides recorded between 1992 and 1998, 16 victims worked for the USPS). The report also concluded that 14 out of the 15 perpetrators of postal acts of violence (since 1986) had histories of violence or mental health issues, and five showed behaviours that, in the opinion of the report, should have excluded them from ever being hired in the first place.[20]

Regardless of whether the reputation was deserved, *going postal* entered the vocabulary and widened to describe any incident of public rage. The *Oxford Dictionary of English Idioms* cites an example from the *New Yorker* in 1999 where a train passenger "'*went postal*' when the battery on his cell phone gave out" with the result that, "A heavyset passenger had to sit on the man until the train finally pulled into Grand Central."[21] The phrase entered popular culture as well: a controversial video game series involving acts of random violence began with *Postal* in 1997, leading to multiple sequels and spin-offs, and even a movie adaptation. (The USPS sued the creators, objecting to the use of the term in association with such a gratuitously violent game, but the case was dismissed in 2003.) Terry Pratchett even used *Going Postal* as the title of one of his Discworld novels in 2004, with a subsequent 2010 TV adaptation.

To redress the balance, *Going Postal* has also been used as the title of a monthly YouTube show on the topic of stamps and postage history. Host Henry Lukas from the Spellman Museum of Stamps and Postal History (based in Weston, Massachusetts) presents a lovingly created show, featuring historical facts, important events in stamp history and "just some very interesting stories about stamps",[22] which is hopefully just the kind of thing to make the USPS a little less aggrieved, and calm any rising tempers before they can get out of hand.

Jump the couch

To display erratic or frenetic behaviour.

Jump the couch originates from a now infamous episode of *The Oprah Winfrey Show* in May 2005, where movie star Tom Cruise was due to publicise the upcoming release of summer blockbuster *War of the Worlds*. *The Oprah Winfrey Show* was not a place that stars expected a particularly tough grilling, but rather was a safe space for celebrities to talk to a kindred spirit and raise their (already pretty healthy) profiles in front of an adoring audience. On this particular occasion, rather than the usual gentle banter and promotional chat, Cruise instead began to rave about the new love of his life, Katie Holmes. His visible enthusiasm, including an uncontrollable smile throughout and a seeming inability to remain in his seat, peaked when he leaped on to the sofa, mock-wrestled with Oprah and finally left the stage to return with a bashful Holmes, all to the adoration of the screaming crowd.

Seen in context, the incident isn't quite as bizarre as it sounds (although it comes close, and is certainly not what Oprah was expecting), but a flood of criticism followed, especially in tabloids and online, where a consensus was that Cruise had well and truly lost the plot. By analogy with the already well-established idiom *jump the shark* (see Chapter 2), denoting the point at which a TV show begins to lose its credibility, *jump the couch* was quickly coined to describe the same happening to a person, based on particularly erratic or unpredictable behaviour. As well as being chosen as Slang Expression of the Year by the *Historical Dictionary of American Slang* (what Today.com dubbed "top gun of slang in '05"),[23] *jump the couch* also quickly made it into the Urban Dictionary in 2005, and was the subject of a blog on the Macmillan Dictionary website in 2006, which gives us other examples of the phrase.[24] Wales rugby union captain Gareth Thomas apparently "*'jumped the couch'* on the BBC, following his side's loss to England", somewhat undermining the argument he was trying to make (that there was no need to panic following the recent departure of Wales Head Coach, Mike Ruddock) in the process. Two retrospective references to *jumping the couch* are also made: to Oliver Reed appearing outrageously drunk on UK chat show *Aspel & Company* in 1987, during which he treated the delighted audience to an incredibly enthusiastic display of dancing; and the "hysterical" behaviour of then Labour party leader Neil Kinnock in the run-up to the 1992 UK general election, when his overconfident performance at a rally in Sheffield just one week before polling day is seen in some quarters as having contributed to a surprise loss in the eventual vote.

Ten years after the original Tom Cruise incident plenty of entertainment writers took the opportunity to recall this as a significant turning point for Cruise and his public image. An article on the Ringer website in 2018 ("The *Couch Jump* That Rocked Hollywood")[25] even went as far as to claim that this was a game changer for celebrity reporting in general, coinciding with a rise in gossip bloggers, Internet commentary and the sharing of things via sites like YouTube, as well a general shift toward a more critical and unforgiving approach from the media. The "real legacy" of the incident was claimed to be the reaction it provoked online, which seems par for the course in today's world of instant reporting and outrage, but which, at the time, transformed the way that celebrities were expected to engage with their public.

Mental safari

A period of brief insanity; a series of rash or stupid actions.

A *mental safari* is a brief period when a person might be described as having temporarily taken leave of her or his senses. This particular phrase can be directly attributed to comedian Alex Horne, who included it in his 2010 book *Wordwatching*, where he relates his mission to introduce a series of new words into common usage.[26] His motivation was simple: he had always loved language, and his ambition was to leave his "linguistic mark on the world" by creating (and establishing in the dictionary) a new word, which turned out to be substantially easier said than done, given the high standards that dictionary compilers generally apply to the inclusion of newly coined words. They require evidence of multiple and prolonged usage, to ensure that a word or phrase is around to stay. So began Horne's "Verbal Gardening Project", where, with the aid of an anonymised committee of helpers, he created and entered into circulation a series of newly coined (or repurposed) words, aiming to spread them far and wide so that at least one could become established enough to qualify as a fully-fledged new word. (As an aside, "verbal gardening" could itself be considered a possible new idiom, but since Alex Horne and his friends seem to be the only ones engaging in this practice, it is perhaps a little premature to be adding this one.) Of course, as a comedian and broadcaster, Alex Horne was in a better position than some to sow his "verbal seeds", and successfully managed to use his new words during radio and TV interviews, in multiple newspaper columns, and at his very own Edinburgh Festival show on the topic in 2008.

Mental safari is the only one of Alex Horne's neologisms to be made up of more than one word, and as Horne himself points out, the meaning is fairly easy to grasp even if it has never been heard before. He describes it as more of a "novel metaphor" than a completely new word, and suggests that this means it should be easy to slip into conversation without raising any eyebrows. To prove this point, he managed to use it successfully during an interview on Radio 4's *Loose Ends*, suggesting at least that his theory about people easily getting the gist is correct. Although his quest to persuade dictionary authorities to include this and his other entries has (at the time of writing) been unsuccessful, *mental safari* does at least have an entry in the Urban Dictionary. Here, it is claimed that *safari* on its own has the slang meaning of a chaotic situation, with a *mental safari* defining stupid behaviour by someone.[27] It does claim (albeit without any supporting evidence) that the term was coined by a college student from Narrabundah (a suburb of Canberra, Australia) in 2009, although since Alex Horne's first foray with the term was on a message board in 2006, this might be best interpreted as a case of parallel linguistic evolution, rather than anything more underhand. Despite the lack of an official entry, Macmillan Dictionary Blog did at least discuss the verbal gardening project and some of its seeds, including *mental safari*, even equating it to another modern idiom in suggesting, "If Tom Cruise can *jump the couch*, there's no reason why you can't go on a *mental safari*."[28]

Not rocket science

Used to suggest that something is relatively straightforward and uncomplicated.

There is no unequivocal source for the use of *not rocket science* to denote something straightforward and not particularly taxing, but it qualifies as "modern" for the fairly obvious reason that rocket science is, by necessity, a relatively modern pursuit, and has only existed as a widespread concept since the middle of the 20th century. Rockets themselves have existed for far longer and probably date back to the use of gunpowder by the Chinese some 800 years ago, but fast forward to the 19th and 20th centuries and interest in the use of rockets to enable spaceflight and improved military applications really picked up speed. The emergence of rocket science as synonymous with great intelligence dates to the end of World War II, when German scientists who had helped to develop a range of rocket powered missiles were captured by the Allies and transported to the USA (as well as the other Allied countries) where their expertise was put to work. The influence of these groups is often credited with enabling and kick-starting the space race between the USA and the USSR, with German scientists on both sides contributing greatly to the development of the technology.

Despite rocket science itself emerging as a byword for a challenging pursuit at this point, The Phrase Finder website suggests that the use of *it's not rocket science* to denote a straightforward task was not actually recorded until some decades later.[29] It reports the earliest instance as coming from a headline in the Pennsylvania-based *Daily Intelligencer* in December 1985, which declared that, "Coaching football *is not rocket science* and *it's not brain surgery*. It's a game, nothing more." There is certainly plenty of suggestion that rocket science replaced the earlier brain surgery in the pecking order of difficult professions, although *it's not brain surgery* doesn't seem to date back too much further; the first attested use as a comparison for something easy provided by the Oxford English Dictionary only dates to 1973, in the book *Everything a Woman Needs to Know to Get Paid What She's Worth* by Caroline Bird. Know Your Phrase cites a slightly earlier example, but only by two years, suggesting that neither phrase is more than a few decades old.[30]

Nowadays, rocket science is the more established, and the TV Tropes website suggests a fairly subtle distinction between the two phrases: whereas *not rocket science* is more likely to be used to indicate that a task doesn't require huge amounts of intelligence, *not brain surgery* is suggested to be more applicable in scenarios requiring precise control and skill. Sometimes people hedge their bets and use both, as in an article from the Canada.com website in 2014 which declared, "Canadian political strategy is not *brain surgery* or *rocket science*, or even *rocket surgery*,"[31] which highlights an even more modern take on the phrase, combining the two to produce the nonsensical but highly entertaining *it's not rocket surgery*. Quite what "rocket surgery" might entail is open to question, and popular culture often suggests this as a classic "Bushism": verbal slip-ups attributed to George W. Bush during his time in office as US President from 2001 to 2009. Bush was known for making such amusing errors (political journalist Jacob Weisberg apparently collated over 500 examples, and he published his top 25 in 2009),[32] but there is no evidence that *not rocket surgery* was one of them. An alternative source, or at least a name that seems to be regularly associated with this portmanteau phrase, is Canadian ice hockey commentator Don Cherry, who is widely reported to have said that "Coaching *ain't rocket surgery*", although a definitive source for this seems to be difficult to locate. More recently, American writer and expert on web usability Steve Krug used the phrase as the title of his 2009 book *Rocket Surgery Made Easy*, which he used to suggest that most of what goes into designing and building an easy-to-use website is just common sense.

Whatever the preferred version, there is still some room for debate over which of rocket science and brain surgery should be considered the more challenging endeavour. British TV comedy show *That Mitchell and Webb Look* (BBC TV, 2006-2010) pitted the two against each another in a sketch from an episode of its third series. The scene features a self-satisfied man at a party (played by Robert Webb), boasting about his job as a brain surgeon, dismissing all other jobs (doctor, accountant, charity worker) as *not exactly brain surgery* to underline his superiority. He is well and truly put in his place when a new guest arrives (David Mitchell) and, when asked his occupation, reveals that he is a scientist, working mostly with rockets. When Webb tells him that he is a brain surgeon, Mitchell replies dismissively, "Brain surgery? *It's not exactly rocket science,* is it?", which would seem to settle the matter once and for all.

Phone it in

To do something in a half-hearted and uncommitted way.

The origins of *phoning it in* seem to go back (almost) as long as there have been telephones. Ben Zimmer, writing on the Visual Thesaurus website, provides a rundown of the development of the word "telephone" from an initial noun to describe Alexander Graham Bell's newly-patented invention in 1876, to a verb ("to telephone somebody"), to the shortened version "phone" even before the 19th century was out.[33] By extension, if you could "phone" an individual, you could "phone in" to a radio station, in the same way that you could "mail in" to a newspaper. Like other idioms, *phone it in* likely started life in a purely literal sense: most will be familiar with the Hollywood image of a newspaper reporter hurriedly rushing to a phone box to *phone in* a story to an editor. According to the Grammarist website the phrase was in common usage amongst theatre actors by the 1930s, the joke being that for a particularly small role it would be more efficient to *phone it in* rather than turn up to deliver the lines in person.[34] Visual Thesaurus does provide a first use of the phrase in print, cited from a roundly sarcastic 1938 review of the play *Our Town*, by Thornton Wilder. The work was deliberately "metatheatrical", breaking the fourth wall with the audience and presenting a minimalist production in terms of scenery, set and props (there were none!), but the reviewer was distinctly unimpressed, suggesting that the next step would be "to have the actors *phone it in*".

The phrase has now broadened out to describe any kind of below-par or unenthusiastic performance, regardless of whether such a duty could actually be fulfilled by telephone. A variant, *mail it in*, is also fairly common, with the same meaning, namely that an actor/politician/sportsperson is simply going through the motions and fulfilling a duty, rather than performing with the vigour and energy that their fans expect of them. In 2015 a Reddit user asked for suggestions of "the best example of a *'Phoned in'* performance" in movies and was obliged with a list of sub-par turns by stars, and sometimes even whole casts. One user took particular exception to Cameron Diaz's performance in *Annie* in 2014, saying, "that wasn't even *phoned it*, that was texted in. That was telegrammed in." Some actors even acknowledge that approaching some roles with less enthusiasm is an inevitable part of getting older, as Anthony Hopkins was reported to have said in an interview in 2011.[35]

In contrast, Merriam-Webster's Usage Notes provides a comparison of *phone it in* with a similar phrase that has a very different meaning.[36] To *dial it in* or to be *dialled in* is to be extremely focused, so more or less the exact opposite of *phoning it in*. This phrase does seem to have emerged much later (in the 1970s, and in the context of tuning engines, according to Merriam-Webster), and the article cites two examples of people misusing *dial it in* when they meant *phone it in*, showing that the potential for confusion between the two does exist (at least amongst those old enough to remember telephones with rotary dials).

Throw someone under the bus

To sacrifice someone in order to minimise harm or embarrassment to oneself.

To *throw someone under the bus* became a staple of American political journalism during the 2008 presidential primary season. Its prevalence was summed up by journalist David Segal, who described it as the "cliché of the 2008 campaign".[37] Specifically, the phrase describes a political candidate being forced (or choosing) to publicly condemn a former friend or ally who has subsequently become something of an embarrassment.

More generally, *throwing someone under the bus* can be used to refer to betrayal in general, especially with overtones of self-preservation by the person doing the throwing.

Although more common in the USA, the phrase seems to have first emerged in relation to UK politics. The first recorded usage, according to Merriam-Webster online, comes from a June 1982 article in *The Times* by journalist and later Conservative politician, Julian Critchley.[38] The piece was a profile of then UK Prime Minister Margaret Thatcher, describing how victory in the Falklands conflict had transformed her from a dead woman walking to a triumphant and untouchable leader. Critchley described how a mere two months earlier, in an emergency debate in the British Parliament, Thatcher had given "the worst speech of her career". She was, Critchley went on to say, "in deep trouble and the lobbies hummed with the prospect of her departure. President Galtieri [the Argentine General who had precipitated the Falklands crisis] had pushed her *under the bus* which the gossips had said was the only means of her removal." Merriam-Webster does cite three earlier uses (in 1971, 1978 and 1980) of *under the bus* being used to refer to the demise of a political leader, but the additional implication of this being the result of betrayal or subterfuge seems to have emerged later. Fast forward to 2008 and *thrown under the bus* had certainly become a part of the political vocabulary. Whether this is an indication that the 2008 primaries were substantially more cutthroat than had been the case previously is unclear, but linguist Geoffrey Nunberg apparently looked into the coverage and found that over 400 press stories featured the phrase over a six month period. Clearly this did not go unnoticed in the wider press, as an article in the *Pittsburgh Post-Gazette* published on 2nd July 2008 asked, "Is it time to *throw 'under the bus' under the bus*?", on the grounds that it was getting "awfully crowded under that bus".[39]

Alongside politics, the phrase has also developed fairly

common usage in the world of American sports. A high-profile example cropped up during the 2015 "deflate-gate" scandal, where the New England Patriots American Football team were accused of deliberately under-inflating match balls in an attempt to gain an unfair advantage over their opposition. In a press conference four days after the game in which this was alleged to have happened, head coach Bill Belichick disavowed all knowledge, instead directing attention to star quarterback, Tom Brady. As Ben Volin wrote in the *Boston Globe*, although Belichick was the "Patriots' de facto CEO" his response was to "feign ignorance and throw his star quarterback squarely *under the bus*".[40] Ultimately, Brady received a four game ban and the Patriots were fined heavily, but Belichick didn't face any personal repercussions, so perhaps in this instance (for Belichick at least) all was well that ended well. What was striking was the number of journalists who chose to describe Belichick's actions in exactly the same terms, with multiple sources all agreeing that this was a prime example of the practice of *bus throwing*. Phil Thompson, writing in the *Chicago Tribune*, even took the opportunity to publish a rundown of "Great moments in *throwing players under the bus*", suggesting that Belichick's deflection was far from the first and certainly far from the most blatant in US sports history.[41]

Wardrobe malfunction

An unfortunate failure of clothing causing the wearer to be unintentionally exposed.

Wardrobe malfunction entered the language in 2004, although it's fair to say that the thing it described had been going on for quite some time before anyone thought to name it. Justin Timberlake first uttered the phrase during a statement made in response to a rather unfortunate element of the half-time show at Super Bowl 38 (which took place on 1st February 2004), during which he had performed alongside Janet Jackson. A pre-planned routine involved Timberlake joining Jackson on stage in order to perform a duet of the song *Rock Your Body* and culminated in him ripping off a section of her clothes, inadvertently exposing her right breast. Given that the Super Bowl is one of the most watched events in the world, with US viewing figures alone estimated at almost 90 million for that particular year, the scandal caused by "nipplegate", as it was dubbed, was extensive. Some accused Jackson of deliberately orchestrating it as a publicity stunt, and commentators decried it as a sign of worsening moral standards in general, and in entertainment in particular. In turn, the crackdown that was the response of broadcasting watchdogs was seen as an attack on free speech and a sign of increased censorship. Like other events that have inspired phrases in this collection (see *Jump the couch*, this chapter), the timing was an important part of how the scandal grew so quickly. Janet Jackson quickly became the most searched term in Internet history (*The Guinness Book of Records* listed Jackson as such in 2007, as well as the most searched news item in history at the time), and held the accolade of most searched for person of 2004 and 2005. Co-founder of YouTube (which launched the following year), Jawed Karim, even cited this as the moment that he realised that video sharing was about to become the next big thing online.[42]

The term itself is an example of the long tradition of euphemism that is often applied to downplay the seriousness of a situation (think *collateral damage*, for another prime example of such strategic understatement). Timberlake is credited with first usage when he apologised to "anyone [who] was offended by the *wardrobe malfunction* during the halftime performance of the Super Bowl" in a statement released immediately afterward, when the organisers were scrambling to assure the world that the incident had been entirely unintended. Subsequent reporting of the event and the fallout meant that the term was widely repeated, helping it to quickly become a part of the vocabulary of 2004. The American Dialect Society included "nipplegate" (as well as alternative terms "boobgate" and "Janet moment") alongside *"wardrobe malfunction"* – which they defined as "Overexposure in a mammary way" – in its nominations for word of the year in 2004. All of these terms were beaten out by eventual winners "red state"/"blue state"/"purple state", coined for the first time during the 2004 Presidential election, when a purple state became another term for a swing state, or one where levels of support for red Republicans and blue Democrats are similar. *Wardrobe malfunction* did not go away, however, and was subsequently added to several dictionaries, including, in 2008, Chambers 11th edition, which defined it as "the temporary failure of an item of clothing to do its job in covering a part of the body that it would be advisable to keep covered".

Given how celebrity reporting has developed in the years since 2004, it's unsurprising that a search for *wardrobe malfunctions* returns numerous "best of" or "most embarrassing" lists, even if the majority of these are genuine accidents involving ill-timed gusts of wind or other examples of unfortunate timing. One person often credited with more purposeful actions, however, was Jayne Mansfield, Hollywood actress and sex symbol in the 1950s and 60s. As well as being one of the earliest Playboy Playmates, she was well-known for her publicity stunts, which often involved *wardrobe malfunctions* where her breasts were "accidentally" revealed, including one infamous occasion during a dinner party held to welcome Italian actress Sophia Loren to Hollywood. Given the stir that this caused in 1957, we can only imagine what modern reporters and Internet consumers might have made of it.

Water cooler moment
An occurrence of such significance that it provokes widespread discussion amongst co-workers the next day.

In the 1990s, *water cooler moments* were groundbreaking or momentous TV events. In the days when viewers were limited to the choice and scheduling offered by terrestrial television channels, great moments in TV history were viewed by everyone at the same time, hence workplace discussions the next day would often centre around what people had watched the night before whilst gathered around the water cooler. The term does appear in the Collins online dictionary, where variants *"water cooler television"* and *"water cooler conversation"* are also provided. The use of *water cooler conversation*, referring to informal, casual chat amongst colleagues in the workplace, seems to date as far back as the 1960s, when an article in the journal *American Anthropologist* described the practice of idly chatting with workmates, "only because the alternative activity is unpleasant".[43]

Despite this, the sense of *water cooler moment* as a specific, conversation-worthy event seems only to have emerged toward the end of the 20th century. In a lateral-thinking attempt to publicise their business, London-based The Water Delivery Company wrote a blog post about water coolers as "the symbolic location for spontaneous workplace chinwagging".[44] The post also claims that the term *water cooler moment* was coined in the 1990s, "when a disgraced children's television personality sparked off a network of chats by the water coolers in many a work place across the country". They neglect to name the personality (probably a sensible move from a legal standpoint), but their claim about this being a 90s coinage seems to be accurate, since use of the phrase to describe must-see TV and other noteworthy events became fairly regular from this point on (on both sides of the Atlantic Ocean).

Modern methods of viewing have changed the nature of the phenomenon, since must-see TV is no longer delivered at the same time to everyone. Several articles have discussed whether streaming services like Netflix have killed the *water cooler moment* (one *Daily Mail* columnist even announced the death of water cooler TV as far back as 2008, suggesting that major sporting events may be the only surviving example even before on-demand took hold).[45] Despite this, there are signs that the concept may be making a comeback. Social media and live streaming platforms have been touted by some as an opportunity to redefine "digital *water cooler moments*",[46] and some commentators, far from seeing Netflix and others as the enemy, have suggested that the impetus these services have provided in producing high quality, big budget episodic TV have breathed new life into the industry and reignited the concept of *water cooler television*. UK celebrity gameshow *Taskmaster* even featured a challenge for its contestants to create their own *water cooler moment* in 2017. Comedian Sally Phillips took the task quite literally when she pretended to engage in a night of passion with an actual water cooler, which surely provided a talking point for some time to come for anyone present.

X is my middle name

An indication that X (whatever X may be) is a particular forte or interest of the person speaking.

Mike Myers (who has already received honourable mention, see Chapter 3) launched his iconic spy persona, Austin Powers, in the 1997 movie *Austin Powers: International Man of Mystery*, and drew on a time-honoured formula for one of the most memorable lines. During a scene when a file clerk is returning Austin's personal effects, he reads the name "Danger Powers" from a list. Austin corrects him, clarifying, *"Danger's my middle name"*. Perhaps helped by the popularity of the film, nowadays the concept of something being *your middle name* is very familiar, but *X is my middle name* has a surprisingly long-standing history. The Glossographia website provides a detailed explanation, suggesting a first usage as far back as the very start of the 20th century.[47] This earliest written example dates from a

Canadian newspaper from 1902, when the general manager of the Northern Commercial company (which operated in Alaska in the early 20th century) declared that *"fight is my middle name"*, in response to an upcoming "trade war" with a competing company. The phrase certainly seems to be North American in origin, with Glossographia reporting a spike in usage in the 1920s when it "seems to have been a fad at the time", then a steady increase from the 1960s onward, possibly as a result of the single *Trouble is My Middle Name*, recorded by Bobby Vinton in 1962. TV Tropes now lists *"'metaphor' is my middle name"* as a common and time-worn formula, often played for laughs by highlighting an unusual or absurd choice of name (as in the Austin Powers example).

The joke exemplifies a type of modern idiom that has been of great interest to linguists in the past, namely the type of "fill in the blanks" template that can be adapted as the situation requires. The Glossophilia website includes *X is my middle name* in its discussion of "snowclones", which are a kind of cliché or stock phrase that can be creatively repurposed as required.[48] The name "snowclones" was jointly coined by linguist Geoffrey Pullum and economist Glen Whitman, who first proposed it to Pullum in 2004, based on the fact that Pullum considered one of the worst journalistic clichés of this type to be the formula: "If Eskimos have N words for snow, X surely must have M words for Y". These "some-assembly-required adaptable cliché frames for lazy journalists"[49] have since been collected into an evolving database on snowclones.org, curated by Erin O'Connor, as well as a comprehensive list (organised by year of first usage) on Wikipedia.

Whilst *X is my middle name* may be one of the more recognisable examples, other snowclones are just as common and easily understood. Expressions like *X is the new Y* (for example, *Orange is the New Black*), *the mother of all X* (Saddam Hussein famously described the first Gulf War as *"the mother of* all battles"), *you're gonna need a bigger* X (see *You're gonna need a bigger boat*, Chapter 3) and *What would X do?* (based on the motto *What would Jesus do?* but now commonly adapted for humorous effect, in examples like *What would Beyoncé do?*) are all part of the repertoire of semi-filled or flexible "templates" that are common in our vocabulary. Other, non-phrasal examples – such as adding the suffix *-gate* on to a word to describe any kind of scandal – also provide easy points of reference that most speakers of English will recognise and understand with little difficulty.

Who can really say why some phrases make it into the wider language while others fall by the wayside? Alongside the ones considered in this chapter, there are many more that could easily qualify as modern idioms, even if we can be less sure of their origins. For instance, who was the first person to tell someone to *talk to the hand* or *wake up and smell the coffee*? Who first told an overly affectionate couple to *get a room*, asked people to *think outside the box* or described the moment when the *shit hit the fan*? All of these can be traced to sometime in the 20th century, but with no definitive record of how or why they first sprang into being. People have been asking *what's the 411?* to obtain relevant information in the USA (411 being the number to dial for directory assistance) since at least the 1980s. More recently, people have begun asking *what's the tea?* to find out the latest gossip; people who do things well or confidently do them *like a boss*; and someone who says something particularly annoying or stupid should *get in the bin*. All of these are now part of our language, even if they may not be as universally recognised as some of the more traditional idioms in circulation.

Perhaps what the examples throughout this collection show us is that creativity doesn't always involve coming up with new ideas from scratch: TV shows, movies and books can contribute their titles or memorable lines to the vocabulary at large, and catchphrases, soundbites and memes can develop well beyond their initial use, showcasing a different kind of innovation and often living on long after the origin has faded into the mists of time. Just like the rest of the idioms we use every day, people don't always need to know the backstory to understand how to use the phrases included in this book, but hopefully it's been fun learning a few.

Notes

1. Introduction: Why Can't People Just Say What They Mean?

1. www.dw.com/en/is-your-pig-whistling-quirky-german-idioms-featuring-pigs/a-47124979
2. www.phrases.org.uk/meanings/kick-the-bucket.html
3. www.georgette-heyer.com/slang.html

2. Don't Touch that Dial: Idioms from the World of TV

1. www.digitalspy.com/tv/ustv/a789050/friends-23-phrases-hit-sitcom-gave-us-we-use-every-day-breezy-friend-zone/
2. www.politico.eu/article/trumps-un-pick-thin-on-foreign-policy-long-on-political-connections-kelly-craft/
3. Who to blame when 'computer says no'. *The Telegraph*, 23rd September 2013.
4. www.manchestereveningnews.co.uk/news/greater-manchester-news/computer-says-no-to-rude-word-1030900
5. Professionals, your time is up, prepare to be sidelined by tech. *New Scientist*, 3rd November 2015.
6. www.dailymail.co.uk/debate/article-2261127/DAILY-MAIL-COMMENT-So-does-say-tin-Mr-Cameron.html
7. Guinness tops advertising slogans most commonly used in everyday life. *The Telegraph*, 19th December 2008.
8. www.lawinsport.com/content/articles/item/football-manager-contracts-of-employment-an-analysis-of-key-clauses-for-clubs-to-consider-part-2
9. www.gq-magazine.co.uk/article/gardening-leave
10. uk.reuters.com/article/uk-britain-powercut/major-power-cut-hits-homes-transport-in-parts-of-britain-idUKKCN1UZ1Z3
11. www.realclearpolitics.com/video/2015/07/20/bill_kristol_donald_trump_jumped_the_shark_hes_dead_to_me.html

12. www.politicususa.com/2016/08/11/cnns-john-berman-ex-plains-abu-bakr-al-baghdadi-founder-isis-obama.html
13. www.theguardian.com/commentisfree/2017/jan/11/don-ald-trump-guantanamo
14. www.stuff.co.nz/entertainment/film/102050845/the-death-of-stalin-armando-iannucci-on-why-his-political-satire-days-are-over
15. www.marketoracle.co.uk/Article23208.html
16. deadline.com/2017/12/barack-obama-prince-harry-interview-social-media-dangers-bbc-meghan-mar-kle-1202232782/
17. simpsonswiki.com/wiki/The_Twilight_Zone
18. H.M. Spencer (1919). In the Twilight Zone. *The Lotus Magazine*, Volume 9, No. 7, pp. 353-359.
19. The curse of University Challenge – why many winners go on to obscurity. *The Telegraph*, 3rd August 2011.
20. www.independent.co.uk/student/news/university-chal-lenge-final-eric-monkman-wolfson-college-cambridge-jer-emy-paxman-a7677406.html
21. R.D. Ramsey (1979). The People Versus Smokey Bear: Metaphor, Argot and CB Radio. *The Journal of Popular Culture*, Volume XIII, No. 2, pp. 338-344.
22. www.mirror.co.uk/3am/celebrity-news/sugababes-and-the-top-10-bands-whose-420315
23. www.comedy.co.uk/tv/only_fools_and_horses/special/catchphrases/
24. www.smh.com.au/entertainment/books/doing-very-nicely-thanks-jan-20041028-gdjzzc.html
25. theculturetrip.com/pacific/australia/articles/why-australi-ans-disown-the-phrase-put-another-shrimp-on-the-barbie/

3. Silver Tongues and Silver Screens: Idioms from the Movies

1. www.afi.com/100years/quotes.aspx

2. Market town claims supermarket plans will 'bleed' town dry. *The Telegraph*, 6th May 2012.

3. hauteliving.com/2019/01/justin-zackham-second-act-bucket-list/665602/

4. www.thebucketlistfamily.com/about

5. www.theguardian.com/lifeandstyle/2012/sep/26/bucket-lists-are-they-good-idea

6. www.independent.co.uk/arts-entertainment/tv/features/glenn-close-lock-up-your-pets-shes-back-1903829.html

7. www.spectator.co.uk/article/diana-the-diva

8. www.standard.co.uk/sport/football/furious-fans-deliver-50kg-of-carrots-to-roma-rabbits-a3127386.html

9. www.nicholascohen.wordpress.com/2017/02/24/the-left-and-the-right-ignored-their-extremists-and-we-ended-up-with-brexit-and-trump/

10. www.esquire.com/uk/culture/tv/a17326/simon-blackwell-explains/

11. www.wordhistories.net/2018/11/27/easy-peasy-origin

12. www.dictionary.com/e/slang/easy-peasy-lemon-squeezy

13. www.npr.org/2007/03/08/7458809/embrace-the-suck-and-more-military-speak

14. slate.com/culture/2012/02/like-groundhog-day-the-misuse-of-a-new-cliche.html

15. The walls are closing in on 'individual #1'. *Financial Times*, 8th December 2018.

16. www.theguardian.com/politics/2019/nov/12/boris-johnson-to-promise-end-to-brexit-groundhoggery-in-first-stump-speech

17. www.vanityfair.com/hollywood/2017/08/bill-murray-groundhog-day-musical-twice

18. www.oregonlive.com/movies/2015/06/do_you_know_where_the_bodies_a.html

19. www.vanityfair.com/news/2017/03/mike-flynn-immunity

20. www.wordhistories.net/2018/05/31/know-bodies-buried

21. www.knowyourmeme.com/memes/nuking-the-fridge
22. www.slashfilm.com/is-nuke-the-fridge-the-new-jump-the-shark/
23. www.overthinkingit.com/2012/02/22/fridge-nuking-scientific-peer-review
24. birthmoviesdeath.com/2013/02/12/nuking-the-fridge-has-nuked-the-fridge-indiana-jones-could-have-survived-af
25. www.inverse.com/article/13127-6-indiana-jones-moments-more-ridiculous-than-nuking-the-fridge
26. filmschoolrejects.com/was-nuking-the-fridge-really-the-most-ridiculous-thing-indiana-jones-ever-did-56b829aaa859/
27. www.digitalspy.com/movies/a347686/steven-spielberg-i-was-against-aliens-in-indiana-jones-4/
28. www.grammarphobia.com/blog/2011/12/sleeping-with-the-fishes
29. www.theringer.com/movies/2018/4/24/17261506/sliding-doors-20th-anniversary
30. www.news.com.au/entertainment/celebrity-life/royals/dianas-sliding-doors-moment-how-princess-life-was-ruled-by-chance-decisions/news-story/30bc740cd68c30d56651f0f1635d11f1
31. www.theguardian.com/sport/2019/apr/16/the-joy-of-six-sporting-sliding-doors-moments
32. travelbaseonline.com/travel/most-brits-have-had-a-sliding-doors-moment-that-changed-their-life/
33. ordinary-times.com/2013/10/20/take-two-red-pills-call-me-in-the-morning-the-sudden-and-surprising-rise-of-the-mens-rights-movement/
34. Welcome to the Red Pill: The angry men's rights group that 'knows what women want'. *The Telegraph*, 13th November 2015.
35. www.businessinsider.com/why-clean-eating-could-be-harmful-to-health-2017-7

36. www.yahoo.com/entertainment/blogs/movie-talk/11-11-11-nigel-tufnel-day-185526454.html

37. www.hollywoodreporter.com/lists/star-wars-jaws-22-films-are-famously-misquoted-1002147

38. www.phrases.org.uk/meanings/the-usual-suspects.html

39. www.npr.org/2016/03/07/469209254/decades-later-spy-magazine-founders-continue-to-torment-trump?t=1567940518170

40. www.hollywoodreporter.com/news/jaws-bigger-boat-quote-writer-872226

41. www.tvtropes.org/pmwiki/pmwiki.php/Main/DramaticDeadpan

42. www.theguardian.com/books/2018/may/31/word-of-the-week-steven-poole-spygate

43. www.mentalfloss.com/article/63573/10-swingingest-austin-powers-slang-terms

4. Breaking the Internet: Idioms from the Online World

1. Richard Dawkins (1976). *The Selfish Gene*. Oxford University Press.

2. www.bbc.co.uk/news/newsbeat-49604745

3. priceonomics.com/we-analyzed-every-meme-on-the-internet/

4. www.merriam-webster.com/words-at-play/break-the-internet

5. www.csmonitor.com/Technology/2011/0927/Google-confirms-that-Googling-Google-won-t-break-Internet

6. www.webbyawards.com/winners/2016/special-achievement/break-the-internet-award/kim-kardashian-west/

7. time.com/collection-post/3587943/things-that-broke-the-internet/

8. www.thewikigame.com/

9. www.sixdegreesofwikipedia.com/

10. www.urbandictionary.com/define.php?term=collateral%20

misinformation

11. www.lexico.com/en/definition/first_world_problem
12. G.K. Payne (1979). Housing: Third World Solutions to First World Problems. *Built Environment*, Volume 5, No. 2, Lessons From the Third World, pp. 99-110.
13. www.nzherald.co.nz/nz/news/article.cfm?c_id=1&objectid=10839171
14. www.buzzfeed.com/omarvillegas/truly-devastating-first-world-problems
15. www.scmp.com/article/300868/voyage-discovery-combatants-go-water
16. www.knowyourmeme.com/memes/first-world-problems
17. www.theguardian.com/commentisfree/2012/oct/09/firstworldproblems-ad-campaign-new-ground
18. www.mirror.co.uk/news/uk-news/celebrity-firstworld-problems-little-things-seem-4080519
19. www.mirror.co.uk/lifestyle/family/should-stop-using-firstworldproblems-hashtag-4941353
20. www.wired.com/1994/10/godwin-if-2/
21. www.newstatesman.com/blogs/fourth-estate/2009/11/50p-tax-160-kulaks-stalin
22. jewcy.com/jewish-arts-and-culture/i_seem_be_verb_18_years_godwins_law
23. Internet rules and laws: the top 10, from Godwin to Poe. *The Telegraph*, 23rd October 2009.
24. www.urbandictionary.com/define.php?term=Keyboard%20Warrior
25. bravewords.com/news/wwiii-frontman-mandy-lion-neither-i-nor-anyone-else-in-this-business-would-be-anything-unless-the-fans-make-us-into-someone-hear-that-axl
26. www.theguardian.com/news/2017/sep/08/lauri-love-british-hacker-anonymous-extradition-us
27. www.channelnewsasia.com/news/asia/hong-kong-protests-wikipedia-keyboard-warriors-police-carrie-

lam-12134978

28. www.opendemocracy.net/en/participation-now/myth-of-keyboard-warrior-public-participation-and-38-degrees/

29. www.urbandictionary.com/define.php?term=Milkshake%20Duck

30. www.lifehacker.com.au/2018/01/top-5-milkshake-ducks/

31. www.theguardian.com/technology/2018/oct/09/himtoo-metoo-tweet-pieter-hanson-mothers-attack-on-feminism-movement-goes-wrong

32. www.thenib.com/the-rise-and-fall-of-milkshake-duck

33. www.theguardian.com/media/shortcuts/2015/sep/29/how-netflix-and-chill-became-code-for-casual-sex

34. graziadaily.co.uk/relationships/dating/netflix-chill-took-internet-ruined-things-everybody/

35. www.dictionary.com/e/slang/netflix-and-chill

36. towardsdatascience.com/ok-boomer-escalated-quickly-a-reddit-bigquery-report-34133b286d77

37. www.independent.co.uk/news/world/americas/ok-boomer-bob-lonsberry-n-word-baby-dictionary-radio-a9186396.html

38. www.vox.com/2019/11/19/20963757/what-is-ok-boomer-meme-about-meaning-gen-z-millennials

39. www.theguardian.com/world/commentisfree/2019/nov/09/my-ok-boomer-comment-in-parliament-symbolised-exhaustion-of-multiple-generations

5. Jumpers for Goalposts: Idioms from the World of Sport

1. www.merriam-webster.com/words-at-play/7-idioms-from-american-football

2. boycott.gdb.me/quotes

3. www.theguardian.com/sport/2004/jul/04/cricket.features2

4. David Deacon, Peter Golding & Michael Billig (1998). Between fear and loathing: National press coverage of the

1997 British general election. *British Elections & Parties Review*, Volume 8, No. 1, pp. 135-149.

5. www.bbc.co.uk/programmes/articles/5tcC9qRjZjc CD75C6G2KCLR/15-of-the-most-poetic-phrases-from-the-beautiful-game

6. www.newmediacampaigns.com/blog/keeping-a-deep-bench

7. www.newyorker.com/humor/borowitz-report/north-korean-government-reassures-citizens-deep-bench-brutal-madmen

8. www.mirror.co.uk/sport/football/news/premier-leagues-worst-flat-track-12937512

9. www.smh.com.au/opinion/sports-clubs-stuart-ayres-and-the-billiondollar-stadium-20160412-go4dog.html

10. www.independent.ie/business/technology/steve-dempsey-tune-in-to-see-facebook-fight-tv-36116703.html

11. www.grammarist.com/idiom/go-big-or-go-home

12. www.barrypopik.com/index.php/new_york_city/entry/go_big_or_go_home

13. www.barrypopik.com/index.php/new_york_city/entry/go_hard_or_go_home

14. www.forbes.com/sites/willhayes/2015/05/13/dont-go-big-or-go-home/

15. Sir Alex Ferguson: I only used the 'hairdryer' six times in 27 years at Manchester United. *The Telegraph*, 10th November 2016.

16. www.theguardian.com/commentisfree/2013/may/09/alex-ferguson-hairdryer-treatment-politics

17. www.independent.ie/entertainment/television/fights-camera-action-vincent-browne-calls-it-a-day-35903628.html

18. www.mirror.co.uk/news/uk-news/david-camerons-key-errors-during-5410145

19. www.football365.com/news/clive-tyldesley-for-f365-football-should-not-ape-parliament

20. www.bbc.co.uk/news/magazine-20464371

21. Dislocated Goalposts. *New Scientist*, January 1976 (Volume 69, No. 983, p. 144). Retrieved from Google Books, 29/08/2019.

22. www.birminghammail.co.uk/sport/football/football-news/barry-fry-birmingham-city-leak-13062683

23. www.theguardian.com/football/2009/sep/25/kim-christensen-admits-moving-goalposts

24. www.nytimes.com/1990/10/28/magazine/on-language-moving-the-goalposts.html

25. www.idiomation.wordpress.com/tag/move-the-goal-posts/

26. Moving the Goal Posts. *The New York Times*, 21st November 2011.

27. languagecaster.com/football-phrase-park-the-bus/

28. web.archive.org/web/20161114230540/http://www.thefootballsupernova.com/2012/06/myth-of-parking-bus.html

29. www.bbc.co.uk/sport/football/27182818

30. www.thesouthafrican.com/news/mid-term-budget-speech-there-is-no-anc-urgency-for-economic-transformation/

31. Mark Wyatt & Glenn Hadikin (2015). 'They parked two buses': A corpus study of a football expression: Using corpus methods to gain insights into the development of popular phrases. *English Today*, Volume 31, No. 4, pp. 34-41.

32. www.irishtimes.com/sport/soccer/english-soccer/joy-of-six-david-de-gea-s-heroics-keep-united-on-winning-run-1.3756639

33. www.theguardian.com/football/2019/jun/09/shelley-kerr-scotland-england-erin-cuthbert

34. www.urbandictionary.com/define.php?term=Squeaky%20bum%20time

35. www.tnp.sg/sports/football/neil-humphreys-reds-wobble-stops-now

36. www.irishcentral.com/business/ireland-being-picked-on-by-eu-says-tim-cook-apple-boss

37. www.theregister.co.uk/2016/10/26/apple_wait_wait_iphone7plus/
38. www.dailymail.co.uk/news/article-1254477/David-Cameron-denies-squeaky-bum-time-poll-reveals-Gordon-Brown-stay-No10-election.html
39. www.barrypopik.com/index.php/new_york_city/entry/take_one_for_the_team
40. www.thea-blast.org/top-stories/2013/11/13/band-kicked-field
41. sea.ign.com/star-wars-4/156330/feature/igns-staff-reviews-star-wars-the-rise-of-skywalker
42. www.bbc.co.uk/sport/football/51090816

6. Doing it by the Book: Idioms from Modern Literature

1. David Crystal (2010). *Begat: The King James Bible and the English Language*. Oxford University Press.
2. www.theguardian.com/uk/2008/jan/28/britishidentity.johncrace
3. www.phrases.org.uk/meanings/mad-as-a-hatter.html
4. theweek.com/articles/468355/10-whimsical-words-coined-by-lewis-carroll
5. www.smithsonianmag.com/history/most-loved-and-hated-novel-about-world-war-I-180955540/
6. ebury.com/e-blog/blog/ebury_post/20194-european-central-bank-meeting
7. www.theguardian.com/books/2007/nov/17/classics.margaretatwood
8. www.inverse.com/article/8924-it-s-a-brave-new-world-for-a-brave-new-world
9. www.dailywritingtips.com/brave-new-world/
10. www.heraldscotland.com/news/18072189.life-age-disinformation/
11. au.eurosport.com/football/premier-league/2019-2020/live-west-ham-united-tottenham-hotspur_mtc1112849/live.shtml

12. A classic by any other name. *The Telegraph*, 18th November 2007.
13. www.theguardian.com/books/2011/oct/10/catch-22-50-years-joseph-heller
14. www.propertyweek.com/feedback/housing-were-in-a-catch-22-situation/5103667.article
15. www.theatlantic.com/international/archive/2019/06/boris-johnson-jeremy-hunt-brexit-catch-22/592258/
16. www.psychologytoday.com/us/blog/in-love-and-war/201204/psychological-catch-22s
17. www.dailydot.com/parsec/lue-message-board-gamegaqs/
18. towelday.org/
19. web.archive.org/web/20080723051103/http://www.scifi.com/sfw/interviews/sfw19051.html
20. www.bl.uk/romantics-and-victorians/articles/arthur-co-nan-doyle-the-creator-of-sherlock-holmes-the-worlds-most-famous-literary-detective
21. www.guinnessworldrecords.com/news/2012/5/sherlock-holmes-awarded-title-for-most-portrayed-literary-human-character-in-film-tv-41743
22. content.time.com/time/magazine/article/0,9171,752005,00.html
23. www.realclearpolitics.com/articles/2006/12/captain_obvious_to_the_rescue.html
24. *Chemical Warfare Bulletin*, Volume 12, No. 8, p. 8 (published 1926). Accessed 18/01/2020 via Google Books.
25. www.science20.com/science_20/gus_grissom_and_liberty_bell_7_50_years_ago_today-81075
26. www.wordorigins.org/big-list-entries/screw-the-pooch?rq=screw%20the%20pooch
27. slate.com/human-interest/2014/01/screw-the-pooch-ety-mology-of-the-idiom-dates-back-to-nasa-and-the-military.html
28. www.salon.com/2014/07/26/strange_bedfellows_putin_

the_chomskyite_left_and_the_ghosts_of_the_cold_war

29. www.gizmodo.com.au/2017/08/game-of-thrones-cut-a-scene-that-would-have-explained-that-winterfell-twist-but-in-a-crappy-way/

30. www.wordorigins.org/big-list-entries/right-stuff?rq= the%20right%20stuff

31. www.independent.co.uk/arts-entertainment/music/features/sophies-choice-auschwitz-and-arias-134317.html

32. www.cbc.ca/news/politics/donald-trump-never-trump-republicans-conservatives-hillary-clinton-support-1.3567944

33. www.dailyrecord.co.uk/news/politics/tory-leadership-race-been-like-16776875

34. www.theatlantic.com/technology/archive/2014/07/a-quest-to-find-the-secret-origins-of-lost-video-game-levels/373925/

35. entertainment.ie/cinema/movie-news/best-movie-soundtracks-2010s-430461/

36. www.theguardian.com/politics/2003/aug/05/davidkelly.huttonreport1

37. www.bbc.co.uk/news/magazine-38085998

7. The Best of the Rest

1. This cap on bankers' bonuses is like a dead cat – pure distraction. *The Telegraph*, 3rd March 2013.

2. www.theguardian.com/politics/2016/jan/20/lynton-crosby-and-dead-cat-won-election-conservatives-labour-intellectually-lazy

3. www.prospectmagazine.co.uk/politics/dead-cat-strategy-meme-meaning

4. www.huffpost.com/entry/trumps-dead-cats_b_583da465e4 b04e28cf5b8bb2

5. www.investopedia.com/terms/d/deadcatbounce.asp

6. www.csmonitor.com/USA/Politics/Politics-Voices/201 6/1031/Speaking-Politics-phrase-of-the-week-dead-cat-

bounce

7. slate.com/human-interest/2015/01/is-the-phrase-drink-the-kool-aid-offensive-because-of-jonestown.html

8. jonestown.sdsu.edu/?page_id=16584

9. jonestown.sdsu.edu/?page_id=67782

10. www.forbes.com/sites/bruceweinstein/2018/03/29/two-great-reasons-to-stop-saying-i-drank-the-kool-aid/#648acd0334e3

11. www.forbes.com/sites/brettnelson/2012/03/15/and-the-winner-of-the-most-annoying-business-jargon-tournament-is/?sh=45c98def3d16

12. www.slate.com/blogs/browbeat/2013/01/25/a_history_of_the_mic_drop_when_did_people_start_dropping_the_mic.html

13. www.nbcnews.com/video/the-ronald-reagan-mic-drop-moment-at-the-1984-debate-771169347862

14. www.bbc.co.uk/news/technology-35941806

15. hellogiggles.com/love-sex/relationships/friends-with-benefits-stories/

16. www.bustle.com/articles/73764-can-friends-with-benefits-turn-into-more-only-for-15-of-people-says-new-study

17. www.huffingtonpost.co.uk/entry/friends-with-benefits_uk_5d52e1b5e4b0c63bcbee0711

18. Violence at work tied to loss of esteem. *St. Petersburg Times*, 17th December 1993.

19. The Year in Review 1993. *Los Angeles Times*, 31st December 1993.

20. Report of the United States Postal Commission On a Safe and Secure Workplace, August 2000.

21. John Ayto (2009). *Oxford Dictionary of English Idioms* (3rd edition). Oxford University Press.

22. www.youtube.com/channel/UCV5-7MRRK-ND-k93RnX-i7pQ

23. www.today.com/popculture/jump-couch-top-gun-slang-

05-wbna10650547

24. www.macmillandictionary.com/buzzword/entries/jump-the-couch.html

25. www.theringer.com/tv/2018/8/1/17631658/tom-cruise-oprah-couch-jump

26. Alex Horne (2010). *Wordwatching: One Man's Quest for Linguistic Immortality*. Virgin Books.

27. www.urbandictionary.com/define.php?term=Safari

28. www.macmillandictionaryblog.com/get-your-paddles-off-my-honk

29. www.phrases.org.uk/meanings/its-not-rocket-science.html

30. www.knowyourphrase.com/it-s-not-brain-surgery

31. o.canada.com/news/national/den-tandt-liberals-offer-canadians-a-fresh-face-new-approach-without-the-whiplash

32. slate.com/news-and-politics/2009/01/the-top-25-bushisms-of-all-time.html

33. www.visualthesaurus.com/cm/wordroutes/mailbag-friday-phoning-it-in/

34. grammarist.com/idiom/phone-it-in/

35. ew.com/article/2011/05/04/anthony-hopkins-thor-phoning-it-in/

36. www.merriam-webster.com/words-at-play/phone-it-in-vs-dialed-in

37. Time to hit the brakes on that cliché. *The Washington Post,* 2nd April 2008.

38. www.merriam-webster.com/words-at-play/why-do-we-throw-someone-under-the-bus

39. www.post-gazette.com/lifestyle/2008/07/02/Is-it-time-to-throw-under-the-bus-under-the-bus/stories/200807020191

40. www.bostonglobe.com/sports/2015/01/22/bill-belichick-message-don-blame-for-deflategate/JjltLRRkse07jqk-pQK4E9I/story.html

41. www.chicagotribune.com/sports/chi-under-the-bus-20150122-story.html

42. variety.com/2018/music/news/remembering-justin-timber-lake-janet-super-bowl-nipplegate-1202683090/

43. Susan Ervin-Tripp (1964). An Analysis of the Interaction of Language, Topic, and Listener. *American Anthropologist*, Volume 66, No. 6, pp. 86-102.

44. www.thewaterdeliverycompany.com/2009/06/26/a-water-cooler-moment/

45. www.dailymail.co.uk/mailonsunday/article-1045957/Death-TV-water-cooler-moment.html

46. www.campaignlive.co.uk/article/create-water-cooler-moment-live-social-broadcasting/1360106

47. glossographia.wordpress.com/2013/08/02/figurative-is-my-middle-name/

48. www.glossophilia.org/?p=4718

49. itre.cis.upenn.edu/~myl/languagelog/archives/000350.html

ACADEMIC AND SPECIALIST

Iff Books publishes non-fiction. It aims to work with authors and titles that augment our understanding of the human condition, society and civilisation, and the world or universe in which we live.
If you have enjoyed this book, why not tell other readers by posting a review on your preferred book site.
Recent bestsellers from Iff Books are:

Why Materialism Is Baloney
How true skeptics know there is no death and fathom answers to life, the universe, and everything
Bernardo Kastrup
A hard-nosed, logical, and skeptic non-materialist metaphysics, according to which the body is in mind, not mind in the body.
Paperback: 978-1-78279-362-5 ebook: 978-1-78279-361-8

The Fall
Steve Taylor
The Fall discusses human achievement versus the issues of war, patriarchy and social inequality.
Paperback: 978-1-78535-804-3 ebook: 978-1-78535-805-0

Brief Peeks Beyond
Critical essays on metaphysics, neuroscience, free will, skepticism and culture
Bernardo Kastrup
An incisive, original, compelling alternative to current mainstream cultural views and assumptions.
Paperback: 978-1-78535-018-4 ebook: 978-1-78535-019-1

Framespotting
Changing how you look at things changes how
you see them
Laurence & Alison Matthews
A punchy, upbeat guide to framespotting. Spot deceptions and
hidden assumptions; swap growth for growing up. See and be free.
Paperback: 978-1-78279-689-3 ebook: 978-1-78279-822-4

Is There an Afterlife?
David Fontana
Is there an Afterlife? If so what is it like? How do Western ideas
of the afterlife compare with Eastern? David Fontana presents the
historical and contemporary evidence for survival of
physical death.
Paperback: 978-1-90381-690-5

Nothing Matters
a book about nothing
Ronald Green
Thinking about Nothing opens the world to everything by
illuminating new angles to old problems and stimulating new
ways of thinking.
Paperback: 978-1-84694-707-0 ebook: 978-1-78099-016-3

Panpsychism
The Philosophy of the Sensuous Cosmos
Peter Ells
Are free will and mind chimeras? This book, anti-materialistic but
respecting science, answers: No! Mind is foundational
to all existence.
Paperback: 978-1-84694-505-2 ebook: 978-1-78099-018-7

Punk Science
Inside the Mind of God
Manjir Samanta-Laughton
Many have experienced unexplainable phenomena; God, psychic
abilities, extraordinary healing and angelic encounters. Can
cutting-edge science actually explain phenomena
previously thought of as 'paranormal'?
Paperback: 978-1-90504-793-2

The Vagabond Spirit of Poetry
Edward Clarke
Spend time with the wisest poets of the modern age and of the
past, and let Edward Clarke remind you of the importance of
poetry in our industrialized world.
Paperback: 978-1-78279-370-0 ebook: 978-1-78279-369-4

Readers of ebooks can buy or view any of these bestsellers by
clicking on the live link in the title. Most titles are published in
paperback and as an ebook. Paperbacks are available in traditional
bookshops. Both print and ebook formats are available online.
Find more titles and sign up to our readers' newsletter at
http://www.johnhuntpublishing.com/non-fiction
Follow us on Facebook at
https://www.facebook.com/JHPNonFiction
and Twitter at https://twitter.com/JHPNonFiction